THE
LEADER'S
SHADOW

THE
LEADER'S
SHADOW

Exploring
and
Developing
Executive
Character

William Q. Judge

SAGE Publications
International Educational and Professional Publisher
Thousand Oaks London New Delhi

For information:

SAGE Publications, Inc.
2455 Teller Road
Thousand Oaks, California 91320
E-mail: order@sagepub.com

SAGE Publications Ltd.
6 Bonhill Street
London EC2A 4PU
United Kingdom

SAGE Publications India Pvt. Ltd.
M-32 Market
Greater Kailash I
New Delhi 110 048 India

Printed in the United States of America

Library of Congress Cataloging-in-Publication Data

Judge, William Q.
  The leader's shadow: Exploring and developing executive
character / by William Q. Judge.
    p. cm.
  Includes bibliographical references and index.
  ISBN 0-7619-1538-9 (acid-free paper)
  ISBN 0-7619-1539-7 (pbk.: acid-free paper)
  1. Leadership. 2. Executive ability. 3. Chief executive officers.
I. Title.
  HD57.7 .J83 1999
  658.4'092—dc21

                                                          98-40294

This book is printed on acid-free paper.

99 00 01 02 03 04 05 7 6 5 4 3 2 1

Acquisition Editor: Marquita Flemming
Editorial Assistant: MaryAnn Vail
Production Editor: Wendy Westgate
Editorial Assistant: Nevair Kabakian
Typesetter/Designer: Christina M. Hill
Cover Designer: Candice Harman

Contents

Part I. Context

Part II. Character of Executive Leaders

Part IV. Conclusions

*To my infant daughter, Anastasia, who trusts me;
even though I frequently put her clothes on backwards.*

*To my toddler son, Colin, who reminds me to play;
even though I often approach life too seriously.*

*To my wife and partner, Sharon, who accepts me;
even though I sometimes find myself unacceptable.*

Preface

There is a problem with existing approaches to leadership and leadership development. Too many theories and training courses focus exclusively on the external aspects of leadership. It is true that leaders influence other people to do extraordinary things and that they even transform entire organizations. However, by focusing on the externalities of leadership, we only get a partial view of what is going on. The source of all these leadership behaviors and competencies is hidden and is often ignored. As a result, leadership development is limited, and human potential is not realized.

I have written this book to challenge conventional leadership thought and to improve leadership development practices by focusing on the complementary, but often ignored, internal aspects of the leadership experience. I am not as pessimistic as some about the prospects for educational institutions to facilitate this type of personal transformation (e.g., Vaill, 1996a). However, I agree with Vaill's assertion that we need to dramatically revamp our approach to management and leadership development so we can better cope with the rapid and unpredictable pace of change as we enter the twenty-first century.

More specifically, I provide a framework for first becoming aware of our own inner landscape; I then offer ideas and exercises for developing our own character. However, this framework is not built exclusively from my own personal experience. Although this is an important first step, anecdotal evidence is limited to specific contexts and can be too easily dismissed as being due to a unique set of circumstances. Therefore, I systematically examine several dimensions of the inner landscape or character of 91 chief executive officers (CEOs) from a wide variety of contexts. In addition, I provide in-depth case studies of seven CEOs to complement the rather broad survey results. These data offer new insights into the inner lives of people in leadership positions, and their enthusiasm and commitment to this research lends further evidence that we have neglected character development for too long.

The Purpose of This Book

In the past two decades, I have become more intensely involved with my own personal growth; and this has led me to an increasing interest in leadership development. Over the most recent decade, I have been a professor of management, teaching students, publishing research, and consulting with industry leaders on various aspects of executive leadership. During this period of time, I have been refining my personal and professional understanding of the concept of leadership, particularly executive leadership. After many blind alleys and dead ends, I am discovering that the development of our own character is central to tapping our own human and leadership potential.

As a result, I wrote this book for several reasons. First, I wanted to address a void in the leadership literature. Too many leadership frameworks and concepts focus on the external aspects of influence and control—or what leaders *do*. This is an unbalanced perspective that ignores the most important part of leadership—which is who the leaders *are*. Certainly, leaders do exercise influence and control in many dramatic ways, but this external focus fails to capture the essential core of leadership—which is all about character.

This external focus on leadership behaviors often confuses leadership activities with the practice of management, and it offers little guidance to others on how to develop their own leadership potential other than encouraging the imitation of others. This internal focus can rebalance the leadership literature and, in so doing, refocus leadership training and development into more productive avenues. In particular,

I encourage others to see that power comes from within, not from mimicking techniques of control or from acquiring "impression management" ideas or from gaining the trappings of prestigious positions. Power comes from being authentic. I agree with the idealistic but wise Randal Franz (1998), who pointedly argues that management educators should be focused more on the character development of their students than on getting them a job.

A second reason for writing this book was to conduct more systematic research than the anecdotal accounts that have been emerging from the popular leadership literature (Northouse, 1997) in recent years, such as *Principle-Centered Leadership* (Covey, 1991) and *Leadership Is an Art* (De Pree, 1987). This literature, which is written primarily for the practitioner audience, has had a large impact on the practice of leadership. Written by consultants and practicing executives, this literature ventures into important areas that most academic writings ignore, such as the creative and spiritual aspects of leadership and the potential to provide life with more meaning.

Although these popular works are invaluable to our understanding, there is a need to build on existing research, to be more precise with our ideas, and to blend descriptive work with some conceptual frameworks (Northouse, 1997). Thus, I approach these ideas in a more systematic and comprehensive way than the previous writers, while building on their seminal ideas.

A final reason why I wrote this book was to force me to consolidate my thinking on a complex phenomenon. I wanted to crystallize my own thinking into a more coherent framework. The scholarly review process does impose a constructive discipline on the writing process, but it also limits creativity and constrains ideas to extant thinking. It is particularly antagonistic to the study of "unobservables" (Godfrey & Hill, 1995)—where most of the insights into leadership exist. Consequently, this venue allows me to be more creative than traditional scholarly work permits.

The central premise of this book is that our leadership potential and ability is an interaction between a specific context and our personal character, and this interaction yields valuable creative fruits within an organization and to our society. Because we have limited control over external forces, we should focus our efforts on those areas where we do have control: our responses to those external forces. However, this is easier said than done. When we start looking sincerely within ourselves, we notice that some parts of our inner being are "illuminated" and easily accessed whereas other parts are "dark" and hidden from view. It is this dark and hidden part of our self, what Carl Jung (1933) calls our *shadow*, that we are required to engage if we want to develop our character, and hence, our leadership potential.

The shadow metaphor is a rich one that is used throughout this book. One assumption that I maintain throughout this book is that we all have a shadow within us, but it does not harm us or others *if* we consciously explore the nature of our shadow and what it is trying to "tell" us. Because our shadow can be both a wellspring of life and a cause of unending pain and suffering, I do not use the term in a positive or negative sense. Consequently, each chapter describes a particular facet of the leader's shadow; but it does not stop there. By way of prescription, I also offer a series of exercises, or "shadow work," for the reader to further explore his or her own shadow.

Brief Overview of the Book

In Chapter 1, I address the concept of the shadow in greater depth. I explore the meaning of this rather cryptic term and relate its importance to the practice of leadership. I address some common misconceptions about the shadow and, at the same time, invite readers to explore the mysterious nature of their own shadow energies. In so doing, we begin to understand that character development is not as straightforward as learning a simple technique or avoiding certain activities. Rather, we learn that shadow work is required by all (especially people aspiring to or in leadership roles); but there is no specific technique that can be followed.

Because each shadow is cast within a specific setting, context is where we start our exploration of leadership. Consequently, Chapter 2 deals with the context surrounding executive leaders. In this chapter, I describe and analyze the industries represented by the CEOs who responded to a survey administered in 1996 (refer to Appendix A for the specific details). Next, I investigate the organizational context surrounding the CEOs by examining such things as organizational size, financial standing, level of diversification, and the CEO's "boss," the board of directors. In addition, we explore the demographic characteristics of the CEOs by reporting such external attributes as gender, age, tenure, and compensation level. Finally, a discussion is provided on each of the seven CEOs who agreed to participate in the field interviews (refer to Appendix B for details on these case studies). These background conditions are the seedbed from which executive character and leadership emerge, so it is an essential starting place.

In this book, we look at three critical aspects of executive character: personality, values, and spirituality. In Chapter 3, we start with an examination of the personalities of executive leaders. Although limited and fairly recent, personality research of executive leaders has been shown to describe and explain their cognitive abilities, emotional intelligence, and social behaviors (Finkelstein & Hambrick, 1996). Using Jungian theory and the popular Myers-Briggs Type Indicator (MBTI) (Myers & McCaulley, 1993), this chapter refines and extends our knowledge about the personalities of executive leaders.

In Chapter 4, values of executive leaders, we begin by examining Robert Haas's proposal that there is a side to leadership that is often not discussed but is essential to leadership effectiveness; this side is personal values. He goes on to say that such values as "trust, autonomy, initiative, industry, identity, intimacy, care and wisdom" must be embraced by all leaders to be effective (Haas, 1992, p. 42). In this chapter, I do not argue for a specific set of values as Haas does; however, I do argue that leaders must be clear about their personal values and live consistently with them—especially when the going gets tough. Using Milton Rokeach's (1973) well-known theory of values as well as his tested and refined "values inventory," we learn about the espoused personal values of executive leaders.

In Chapter 5, we venture into the relatively new and unexplored territory of the spirituality of executive leaders. Max Weber (1920) argued persuasively that the Protestant work ethic was the covert force that provided the growth and energy behind capitalism. This may have been true in the past, but today, executives are increasingly "going public" about the importance of their faith and spiritual journey (Mastony, 1998). Building on Gordon Allport's well-known psychological inventory called the Religious Orientation Scale, we analyze the religious affiliations and orientations of CEOs in this chapter (Allport & Ross, 1967).

But we do not limit our examination of spirituality to only its formal and organized aspects in Chapter 5. We also explore the informal aspects by examining the spiritual beliefs and practices of executive leaders separate from their religious practices. Many writers have previously noted that religiosity is the formal and collective expression of faith, whereas spirituality is the informal and individual experience of faith (e.g., Roof, 1994). Clearly, these two concepts are intertwined but distinct. Michael Novak (1996), the "theologian of capitalism," argues that "business is a calling," with a unique ministry and a special spirituality (p. 1). If this is correct, we need to know what the spiritual inclinations and understandings are for executive leaders. In this chapter, I document what the literature has to say about this emerging subject and explore the spiritual beliefs and practices of the executives who participated in this research.

In addition to their personal shadows, there are also collective shadows that leaders need to recognize and address. With respect to executive leadership, this collective shadow often shows itself in dark expressions of corporate culture. More specifically, I argue that the absence of organizational creativity and innovation is a clear sign of collective shadow at work within an organization.

Unlike management, with its emphasis on handling things in the present, the essence of leadership is an ability to assist in creating the future. Thus, we focus in Chapter 6, "Creating a Vision of the Future," on the ability to imagine the organization's destiny. By summarizing the theory and research surrounding visionary leaders as well as by exploring the personal visions of our research participants, I offer some ideas on how visions can become a guiding and inspiring light to organizational members.

A second creative fruit that marks an effective leader is an ability to balance conflicting stakeholder interests through multiple and disparate strategic goals. Consequently, Chapter 7 deals with creating strategic priorities by executive leaders. Interestingly, in a recent survey of chief financial officers (CFOs), over two thirds of the responding CFOs indicated that their firms recognize the importance and necessity of pursuing multiple financial and nonfinancial goals (Birchard, 1995). In this chapter, we explore the strategic goals and stakeholder orientations of our CEO participants, and we delve into how those important priorities were determined.

A third and final creative fruit that demonstrates leadership is the development and maintenance of trust within and between organizations. In Chapter 8, "Creating Organizational Trust," I focus on the implementation of the vision and priorities of executive leadership. To engender organizational trust, the executive leader must be trustworthy. Trustworthiness stems from competence and integrity, which are additional manifestations of executive character. This section is developed by using theory and research on trust and blending those insights with field research consisting of the reports from the top management team regarding the CEOs' trustworthiness (see Appendix C for further details). In this way, we explore the importance of trust on the part of organizational members to act on the vision and pursue the multiple strategic priorities to overcome organizational inertia and self-interested behavior.

Of course, neither character nor creative fruits manifest independently. In Chapter 9, "Character and Creative Fruits," we examine the interconnectedness of these two aspects. To document these interrelationships, we examine some of the linkages between the executive's personality, values, and spirituality as well as the linkages between executives' character and their creative fruits. In so doing, we discover several interesting and noteworthy relationships.

Finally, in Chapter 10, "Going into the Shadow and Emerging a Leader," I offer some concluding points about the leader's shadow. In so doing, I review and summarize key points in the overall book, suggest a new way of looking at power, and explore the special difficulty that leaders may have with exploring their own shadows. In addition, I offer some additional thoughts on recognizing your shadow and outline the considerable benefits of doing shadow work.

Who May Benefit?

There are three groups of people who can benefit from reading this book and exploring its ideas. First, people who are interested in developing their leadership potential will find the examples and exercises particularly useful. If you think you might like to lead a group of people or an entire organization in the future, this book can assist you in that endeavor by providing exemplars, a conceptual framework, and some developmental exercises to help you prepare for that adventure.

Second, the trainers, consultants, and academics who are charged with assisting others in their leadership development can gain from experimenting with these concepts and ideas. The research cited and ideas advanced will challenge your previous thinking on leadership and can offer new ideas for exploring this subject with others. Furthermore, these ideas can be useful in helping to diagnose organizational problems and provide some insights into workable solutions.

Finally, executives in leadership positions may find these ideas to be a support and challenge to themselves as they discharge their duties. If you feel your organization is failing to keep up with its environment or if your organization seems to be losing its coherence, you can find some useful and interesting ideas in this book to pursue. Furthermore, if you feel you are entering a "dark night of the soul" or what some would call a "midlife crisis," these ideas may help you move through this period and become more alive, more optimistic, and more self-assured.

Having personally grappled with the integration of my inner world with my outer work, I admit that this wrestling match is not for the faint of heart. Indeed, there can be dark and uncertain moments learning about ourselves and what the shadow is conveying to us. However, the rewards of exploring and embracing your shadow are enduring and life giving. Paradoxically, this personal inner work can also benefit those around you, and the fruits of this work can even serve future generations and the larger society as a whole.

Acknowledgments

In a study as large as this one, there are many whose help made the project possible. Major funding came from Consulting Psychologists Press, a private organization located in Palo Alto, California, interested in the study of personality. In addition, their staff provided free and timely assistance in the administration of the personality inventories. To the staff of CPP, my great appreciation.

Many people deserve mention for their help in the development and writing of this book. My research assistant, Jack Wheeler, was instrumental in helping to administer and analyze the survey. Jack's attention to detail and diligent follow-through really made a difference as I tried to juggle all my other responsibilities. My graduate students interested in the subject of leadership were willing to explore new areas of study in unconventional ways. This allowed me to test out my ideas and refine my thinking. And Charlotte Duncan transcribed each and every field interview with accuracy and thoroughness.

While I was writing the manuscript, numerous colleagues read my draft copies and provided extremely useful feedback. Specifically, Peter Vaill, Jeff Cowell, Judi Neal, Martin Rutte, and Robert Burnside critiqued portions of the book, whereas Charley Tack, Ed Stead, and Kent Miller read the entire manuscript from start to finish and provided invaluable feedback. Charlotte Duncan, my friend and writing coach, encouraged me to find my own voice and offered her considerable expertise in writing and rewriting this book. My highly competent and very human editor, Marquita Flemming, and all the people at Sage were professional and enthusiastic throughout the production of this book. Furthermore,

I deeply appreciate Kathryn Jones for sharing her data with me on the perceived trustworthiness of CEOs.

Of course, I am particularly appreciative of all the CEOs who took the time and trouble to answer my questions and share their inner experiences. Without their cooperation, this book would be much more theoretical and frankly, less interesting. And last, but not least, I am grateful to Sharon, my wife, who listened to my ramblings, did extra duty with the children when a deadline approached, and believed in me and my abilities.

Introduction

There is nothing more difficult to take in hand, more perilous to conduct, or more uncertain in its success, than to take the lead in the introduction of a new order of things.
— Machiavelli (1513)

I have a little shadow that goes in and out with me, and what can be the use of it is more than I can see.
— Childhood rhyme of unknown origin

The dictionary defines a shadow as "the dark figure cast upon a surface by a body intercepting the rays from a source of light" (Merriam-Webster, 1983, p. 1080). Consequently, the brighter and more concentrated the light, the darker the figure projected. Shadows are common but somewhat mysterious phenomena. They vary in their size and in their direction depending on the angle of the sun. Also, physical shadows often have a fuzzy or indistinct quality. We often can make out the broad outlines of the object or individual, but we often cannot discern the particular features or individual characteristics (Harris, 1991).

Despite the ubiquity of shadows, they are difficult to study and challenging to understand. Shadows can't be weighed or tested. Fur-

1

thermore, shadows change frequently and are hard to describe. Sometimes, a viewer might not be able to tell whose shadow he or she is viewing because individuals of relatively similar size and shape cast very similar physical shadows (Harris, 1991). It is no wonder we often limit our focus to the object or person rather than its shadow because objects and persons are distinct and tangible and, hence, are more easily observed and described.

Just as people cast physical shadows, they also cast psychological shadows (Jung, 1923, 1933). Psychological shadows can provide much valuable information if we are creative enough to engage them directly in what has been called "shadow work" (Zweig & Wolf, 1997). Unlike conventional work, which focuses on material progress and tangible results, shadow work requires us to go within and learn from our inner being. Implicit to the shadow-work notion is the idea that a shadow is cast inside as well as outside of ourself. Although shadow work is difficult work—some say the most difficult work there is (Bly, 1988; Zweig & Wolf, 1997)—the rewards that stem from it are enormous and ongoing.

Everyone casts a shadow (Zweig & Wolf, 1997), but shadows created by individuals in leadership positions are particularly noteworthy (Palmer, 1994). Due to the glare focused on their elevated positions within organizations, leaders often cast the longest and darkest shadows. The metaphor of a physical shadow is a vivid one that reminds us that even though psychological shadow work requires individual effort, it often affects others in dramatic and unexpected ways. The shadows of those in leadership positions are the focus of this book.

Parker Palmer (1994) defines a leader as "a person who has an unusual degree of power to project on other people his or her shadow, or his or her light" (p. 24). Like our physical shadows, our psychological shadows are often projected unconsciously. Unlike physical shadows, projected psychological shadows can do great harm to others if we are in leadership positions and our shadow is large and unrecognized. In other words, a leader is a person who has the opportunity to shape a group's or an organization's destiny so that the act of leadership can be as illuminating as a clear summer day or as dark as a cold winter night.

In sum, a leader has a special responsibility for what is going on inside himself,[1] lest the act of leadership leads to more harm than good. However, exploring and understanding our shadow can yield dramatic new insights and creative actions (Bly, 1988; Zweig & Wolf, 1997).

Shadows teach us that there are mysterious forces at work in our lives that are most dangerous to us and others only if we ignore them. Put simply, getting to know one's shadow can be liberating whereas ignoring one's shadow can enslave.

Why Another Book on Leadership?

This is a book about executive leaders who have overall responsibility for the survival and prosperity of a business enterprise. Based on a growing number of academic studies and thousands of articles in the business press about executive leadership, we know quite a bit about the outer experience and activities of these individuals. For example, Syd Finkelstein and Don Hambrick (1996) recently published a comprehensive book on many studies regarding what top executives *do* and how those actions affect the overall organization. Similarly, Bernard Bass (1990) has published a third edition of his ever-popular *Handbook of Leadership,* which documents literally hundreds of studies on leadership at all levels of the organization and what the leaders *do.* One of the most popular books on leadership today, *The Leadership Challenge,* written by James Kouzes and Barry Posner (1995), provides numerous practical tips and anecdotes on how to get extraordinary things *done* within organizations.

Despite the many useful and interesting insights of these popular books, there has been minimal, if any, systematic study on the inner experience of *being* a leader of an organization. One of the primary reasons for this is the difficulty of gaining access to these busy executives—chief executive officers (CEOs) just do not have the time to participate with interviewers or fill out lengthy survey instruments, which are the traditional ways of studying inner states of being. Furthermore, there is virtually no publicly available data on the inner life of CEOs. As a result, data collection is very costly, time consuming, and hard to secure.

A second reason for the minimal systematic study of the inner experience of being a CEO is the academic community's interest in being perceived as a "scientific" enterprise (Godfrey & Hill, 1995). The inner life of a CEO is a subjective experience, and what data are collected remain hard to verify using traditional criteria of social science. As a result, it is extremely difficult to be "objective" in one's data collection from the standpoint of traditional social science. Consequently, most academics choose not to study phenomena that go beyond their traditional tools of inquiry.

Recognizing the difficulties and obstacles associated with objective data collection, there are several reasons why we need to know more about the inner experiences of CEOs. *First, there is anecdotal evidence that leaders who know themselves and work with their inner experiences are better suited for the current business environment.* Leaders currently operate in "permanent white water" (Vaill, 1996a), to invoke another vivid metaphor. Progressive individuals and organizations on the cutting edge now recognize the importance of going within. The wellspring of such dimensions as offering creative visions of the future, engendering trust, tolerating dissent and ambiguity, and developing subordinates all are the behaviors being sought by leading organizations, and all are derived from the inner person of the executive leader. In other words, any kind of carefully crafted external image (e.g., acting decisively) or the addition of an additional technique of influence and control (e.g., gaining followers) may be less important than who the leader is inside.

The widespread popularity of the *Dilbert* cartoons documents the lack of trust and respect many workers have for their current leaders. In addition, the leaders themselves recognize that the old ways of leading not only hamper their organizations but are also harmful to themselves. Illustrating this point, a leadership development expert notes,

> Execs who are effective in their jobs and successful in their careers often report an unhappy side effect: Their lives get out of balance with most of their energy devoted to work and little left for family and leisure. The reason for this is that the road to success emphasizes "striving for mastery" while "avoiding intimacy." This emphasis on outer success at the expense of the inner success leads to burnout and ineffectiveness in the long-term. (Kofidomos, 1989, p. 21)

One of the outcomes of all this pressure is the increasing rate of turnover in the executive suite, especially in the CEO position. One study estimates that CEO turnover is at an all-time high in the 1990s, with involuntary dismissals on the increase and average job tenure continuing to shrink from 10 years in the 1980s to 7 years in the current decade (Grube, 1995).

Executive leaders do have unprecedented power to influence many, many lives, but they often admit to enormous limits on that ability. For example, the CEO's discretion is limited by increasingly potent and opinionated outside directors; the threat of legal action in the form of shareholder suits, product liability suits, and employee lawsuits; constant oversight by vigilant news media; and the threat or reality of governmental regulations. Furthermore, an increasingly democratized workplace puts increasing checks and balances on the CEO's authority, and the complexity of a global marketplace and fast-changing technologies often transcend the CEO's knowledge base. Indeed, some even argue that we should abandon the concept of leadership altogether and focus greater attention on effective "followership" (Kelley, 1992).

However, thoughtful observers argue that the leader's new task is to empower others to follow more effectively or to become leaders themselves. To cope with these complex and volatile trends, some observers argue that executive leaders need to tap the "power within" (Haas, 1992). *Fortune* magazine recently published an article entitled "Leaders Learn to Heed the Voice Within," documenting how pioneering leadership development programs are experimenting with new ways to promote the inner awareness of business leaders and to facilitate the connection with one's inner being (Sherman, 1994).

Unfortunately, little is known about the actual inner life of executive leaders; even less is known about how to tap that inner power. Many are still searching fruitlessly for external mastery while ignoring their inner turmoil. Reflecting this difficulty, another leadership development expert noted,

> Leaders are in a bind: they are being asked to behave toward subordinates in ways that run counter to what has made them successful. To escape this bind, leaders must engage in development at the level of personal meaning, and organizations must change into institutions supporting such development. (Drath, 1993, p. 2)

In sum, old practices and models of leadership no longer seem to work. Illustrating the pervasiveness of this reality, Warren Bennis (1990) declared,

Thus, America—having been invented by brilliant political leaders and developed by brilliant business leaders—has no leaders at all today. Instead, we have gamesmen—men and women who are vastly clever and ambitious but have no real understanding or vision. (p. 102)

The second reason for needing to examine the inner aspects of executive leadership is that academic scholars have ignored this dimension as much if not more so than practicing executives. Commenting on his becoming the president of the University of Cincinnati and advising four U.S. presidents, Warren Bennis (1990) discovered that "existing academic theories of leadership were useless" (p. xiv). Similarly, one of the chief complaints from business executives about MBA programs is the lack of leadership ability and self-awareness demonstrated by MBA graduates (Behrman & Levin, 1984; Friedrich, 1981; Fuchsberg, 1990).

Some theorists argue that by conceiving leadership as power and influence over others, we have limited its usefulness and its meaning. In contrast, these same observers argue that the essence of leadership is not power over, but power with (Follett, 1942), or more about service to than command of the followers (Block, 1993; Greenleaf, 1977), or even to be more about loving people than manipulating them (Boulding, 1989). These writers are onto something important. Like Peter Senge (1990), I believe that the reconceptualization of executive leadership starts with self-awareness and continues with a search for "mastery" of one's inner core. In short, the traditional observers and writers about leadership seem to be unable to offer new concepts and ideas for addressing this leadership void. New concepts about executive leadership appear to be needed.

A third reason for needing to know about the inner experience of executive leaders is that some of the greatest breakthroughs in scientific understanding have come from studying phenomena from a different perspective. Thomas Kuhn (1970) observed that all major breakthroughs in scientific discovery came from looking at things differently than the commonly accepted ways. The same may be true about executive leadership—breakthroughs in understanding may result from examining the inner dynamics of strategic leaders rather than the traditional objectivist perspective that looks at external behaviors and conditions.

Indeed, some observers argue that the old paradigm view of leadership is breaking down and no longer serves society well (Harman & Hormann, 1993). In contrast, the new science approach demands examination of subjective phenomena, such as values and vision (Wheatley, 1994). Proponents of the new science argue that inner human experience has replaced the outer human senses as the new test of reality (Ray & Rinzler, 1993). Thus, this book attempts to develop new insights into executive leadership by systematically studying that which is very difficult to study systematically: namely, the subjective inner experience of CEOs.

Illuminating the Executive Leader's Shadow

Consistent with this emphasis on the inner experience of executive leadership, there are some exceptions that have emerged in the recent leadership literature that shed new light on the inner experiences of a few individuals in executive leadership positions. Notably, most of these were published in the 1990s, and all come from firsthand accounts of actual CEOs. For example, Tom Chappell (1993), current CEO of Tom's of Maine, a thriving consumer products firm that competes with Proctor and Gamble, argues persuasively that the chief executive's inner character and beliefs drive strategy and organizational outcomes. Similarly, Richard Hallstein (1992), CEO of an international management consulting firm, offers revealing insights about his inner struggle to break the addiction of wielding power autocratically. Also, James Autry (1991), former CEO of the Meredith Corporation and currently a writer of "business poetry," offers revealing insights into his former hopes and fears as well as his vision of the future.

These recent autobiographical accounts provide our first glimpses into the mysterious world of executive leadership and the inner life of presidents and CEOs. Collectively, these anecdotes inform us that the character of executive leaders matters and is worthy of further investigation. This book is an attempt to be more comprehensive by studying executive leadership over a broader range of individuals than previous anecdotal accounts provide. In addition, each chapter concludes with some developmental exercises that provide guidance for those individuals who are looking for assistance in their shadow work.

In this book, I focus on exploring and developing executive character for leadership positions. To bring this exploration into sharper focus, we will examine the context and character and creative fruits of individuals in prominent executive leadership positions—CEOs. By focusing on executive leaders at the top of the organizational hierarchy, I do not mean to imply that all CEOs are of exemplary character. Furthermore, I do not intend to imply that leadership does not exist outside the CEO's office. However, examining current practices and understanding existing top executives can be illuminating, and the few executive leaders that have done or are doing their shadow work may offer insights and inspiration for others.

Specifically, this book examines CEOs of publicly held corporations. This focus excludes CEOs of privately held business firms as well as general managers in charge of nonprofit and governmental entities. One of the reasons for restricting the study to publicly held firms is that the institutional pressure to ignore one's inner life is the greatest for these individuals. In other words, the external pressure to meet financial targets dwarfs the pressure that exists to explore and/or engage one's shadow. Indeed, CEOs who do their shadow work in these organizations must be deeply motivated and truly committed.

Summing Up

My purpose in writing this book is to explore the character of executive leaders and investigate the contextual antecedents and organizational effects of their character. Using the metaphor of the physical shadow, I conceptualize executive character as a mixture of light and dark that has great potential to harm or benefit the rest of the organization. To explore executive character, one must delve into the mysterious inner core of busy executives. Because the inner cores of individuals vary considerably, we need to explore numerous CEOs so we may become familiar with the landscape of possibilities. Of course, there is no substitute for exploration of our own shadow, and this book offers some insights and exercises for doing so. Perhaps, *Fortune* magazine put it best when one of its writers concluded with the following:

Executives are not an introspective lot, but in the dawn of the New Economy—with no job security or clear career path, with more responsibility and less certainty than ever—stressed out managers are increasingly turning inside for answers. In fast-shifting markets, the unexamined life becomes a liability and an aptitude for continued learning has become a mission critical skill for individuals and organizations. (Sherman, 1994, p. 93)

Note

1. Because the vast majority of CEOs are male, I will use masculine pronouns throughout this book. My apologies to anyone who might be offended by this decision.

PART I

Context

2

Context Surrounding
Executive Leaders

*The trouble with American leaders is that they are not sufficiently
aware of the context of whatever they are responsible for doing.
. . . The conventional view of leadership emphasizes positional
power and conspicuous accomplishment. But true leadership is
about creating a domain in which we continually learn and
become more capable of participating in our unfolding nature. A
true leader sets the stage on which predictable miracles, synchronistic in nature, can and do occur.*
— Joseph Jaworski, 1996, pp. 96, 182

*The organization cannot be managed by "science," that is, we
cannot logically determine what causes will produce what effects.
Therefore, we need faith in our judgment, our intuition, our ability
to understand ourselves and others, all in some broader context.*
— Peter Vaill, 1991, p. 192

We begin our investigation of executive leadership by exploring the
context that surrounds executive leaders. It is the context, or background conditions, that influences and is influenced by executive
leadership. It is helpful to explore and understand what contextual

13

factors confront executive leaders as well as limit their discretion, or latitude of action.

Certain contexts yield considerable degrees of freedom, or discretion, to executive leaders (Finkelstein & Hambrick, 1996). We call these "high discretion" contexts. Other contexts are limiting to strategic leaders. We call these "low discretion" contexts. As Donaldson and Lorsch (1983) astutely argue, "CEOs usually have unlimited ambition, but limited choices" (p. 5). Therefore, it is helpful to understand what contextual factors confront these CEOs and limit their discretion. We begin our exploration by examining the *industry context* of the responding CEOs by describing the primary external environment in which they operate. Next, we explore the *organizational context* within which the CEOs exist. This is then followed by a description of the *demographic characteristics* of the CEOs, to get a better feel for the external attributes of executive leaders. Finally, we conclude with seven case studies of CEOs and describe the *contextual situations* within which they operate.

Industry Context

Industry context has been repeatedly found to influence the behavior or managerial discretion of executive leadership. For example, different industries pose different types and levels of uncertainty (Thompson, 1967), and the nature of that uncertainty will determine which competitive actions succeed and fail within that industry. Because of this contextual variation, we need to know something about the industry context to fully describe and explain executive leadership behaviors and organizational outcomes (Finkelstein & Hambrick, 1996).

As can be seen in Exhibit 2.1, a wide variety of industries are represented by the CEOs who responded to our survey. CEOs from 57 different industries participated in this research. The industries spanned consumer durable goods, nondurable goods, industrial products, and a wide variety of service industries.

Interestingly, the only industry that was heavily represented by our survey respondents was the banking industry, where 22% of our sample were situated. This raises the question: Are CEOs of banks more likely to be interested in and, hence, respond to research surveys about the

Exhibit 2.1 Industry Context for Responding CEOs

Primary Standard Industrial Classification	Industry Name	Frequency	Percent	Distribution
1311	Crude petroleum and natural gas	1	1.1	*
1423	Crushed and broken granite	1	1.1	*
1622	Bridge, tunnel, and elevated highways	1	1.1	*
2013	Sausages and other prepared meats	1	1.1	*
2253	Knit outerwear mills	1	1.1	*
2452	Prefabricated wood buildings	1	1.1	*
2611	Pulp mills	1	1.1	*
2711	Newspapers	1	1.1	*
2821	Plastics materials and resins	1	1.1	*
2824	Organic fibers, non-cellulosic	1	1.1	*
2834	Pharmaceutical preparations	1	1.1	
2842	Polishes and sanitation goods	1	1.1	
2873	Nitrogeneous fertilizers	1	1.1	*
3334	Primary aluminum	1	1.1.	*
3483	Ammunition, except for small arms	1	1.1	*
3531	Construction machinery	1	1.1	*
3556	Food products machinery	1	1.1	*
3567	Industrial furnaces and ovens	1	1.1	*
3571	Electronic computers	1	1.1	*
3661	Telephone and telegraph apparatus	3	3.3	***
3633	Radio and TV communications equipment	1	1.1	*
3829	Measuring and controlling devices	1	1.1	*
4213	Trucking, except local	1	1.1	*
4512	Air transportation, scheduled	1	1.1	*
4813	Telephone communications, except radio	1	1.1	*
4911	Electric services	1	1.1	*
4924	Natural gas distribution	2	2.2	**

(continued)

Exhibit 2.1 Industry Context for Responding CEOs *(Continued)*

Primary Standard Industrial Classification	Industry Name	Frequency	Percent	Distribution
5013	Motor vehicle supplies and new parts	1	1.1	*
5141	Groceries, general line	1	1.1	*
5159	Farm-product raw materials	1	1.1	*
5311	Department stores	1	1.1	*
5331	Variety stores	1	1.1	*
5399	Miscellaneous general merchandise	1	1.1	*
5411	Grocery stores	1	1.1	*
5812	Eating places	2	2.2	**
5999	Miscellaneous retail stores	1	1.1	*
6153	Short-term business credit	1	1.1	*
6162	Mortgage bankers and correspondents	1	1.1	*
6321	Accident and health insurance	1	1.1	*
6331	Fire, marine, and casualty insurance	2	2.2	**
6512	Nonresidential building operators	1	1.1	*
6712	Bank holding companies	20	22.0	********************
7011	Hotels and motels	2	2.2	**
7323	Credit reporting services	1	1.1	*
7372	Help supply services	1	1.1	*
7373	Prepackaged software	1	1.1	*
7374	Data processing and reparation	1	1.1	*
7812	Motion picture and video production	1	1.1	*
8011	Offices and clinics of medical doctors	1	1.1	*
8051	Skilled nursing care facilities	1	1.1	*
8063	Psychiatric hospitals	1	1.1	*
8069	Specialty hospitals, except psychiatric	1	1.1	*
8071	Medical laboratories	1	1.1	*
8711	Engineering services	2	2.2	**
8741	Management services	1	1.1	*
8744	Facilities support services	1	1.1	*

NOTE: Data are from the year 1996. Each * = about 1% of the sample.

inner journey than CEOs of other industries? In other words, is this sample systematically biased toward the banking industry and away from other industries?

To address this question, we compared the distribution of industries from our responding 91 CEOs to the general population of industries represented by 91 nonresponding CEOs. We found that 21% of non-responding CEOs also worked within the banking industry. Because this proportion of nonresponding CEOs was not statistically different from the proportion of responding CEOs, we conclude there is acceptable industry representation in our study and that there is no systematic industry bias. Put more simply, banks simply make up a large number of publicly held corporations, and our sample reflects that fact.

Previous research has shown that the level of industry profitability influences executive discretion (Finkelstein & Hambrick, 1996). Exhibit 2.2 shows there is a considerable range in profitability levels experienced in these industries. For example, the high technology industries, such as computer hardware and software, telecommunications, and pharmaceutical industries, were all high-profit industries. In contrast, the commodity industries, such as mortgage banking, petroleum, and organic fibers industries, were all relatively low-profit industries. These findings are consistent with Balkin and Gomez-Mejia (1987), who reported more executive discretion in high technology industries.

Organizational Context

In addition to the industry context, we know the organizational context also influences and is influenced by strategic leaders (Hambrick & Mason, 1984). Research also shows there are often interrelationships between the organizational characteristics and managerial discretion of executive leaders (Finkelstein & Hambrick, 1996). For example, numerous researchers have found that organizational size is more highly correlated with CEO compensation than organizational performance is (e.g., Sridharan, 1996). Because of this relationship, researchers argue that CEOs have more discretion to influence their jobs and their compensation in larger organizations than in smaller organizations (Finkelstein & Hambrick, 1989).

Research has also shown that the level of board control influences managerial discretion. My own research shows that the proportion of

Exhibit 2.2 Industry Context Sorted by Industry Profitability

Standard Industrial Classification	Industry Name	Industry Return on Assets
7323	Credit reporting services	.112
7373	Computer systems design	.104
7372	Prepackaged software	.097
2834	Pharmaceutical preparations	.094
7374	Data processing	.090
7363	Help supply services	.089
3661	Telephone apparatus	.085
7812	Motion picture production	.085
2711	Newspapers	.084
3829	Measure/Control devices	.082
3531	Construction machinery	.082
8711	Engineering services	.080
5812	Eating places	.080
2842	Organic fibers	.076
3571	Electronic computers	.075
2013	Sausages and other meats	.074
2821	Plastics materials and resins	.073
6153	Short-term business credit	.072
2452	Prefabricated wood buildings	.071
3663	Radio/TV communication equipment	.070
5999	Miscellaneous retail stores, not elsewhere classified	.068
3556	Food products machinery	.066
4813	Telephone communications	.065
8071	Medical laboratories	.065
1622	Bridges, tunnels, highways	.064
4213	Trucking, except local	.064

insiders on the board and the size of the board are inversely correlated with the level of board involvement in the strategic decision-making process (Judge & Zeithaml, 1992). In short, big boards with few independent outside directors are more likely to acquiesce to the CEO's demands and, hence, offer him more discretion.

Similarly, Finkelstein and Hambrick (1996) reported that the organization's financial standing, or "slack" resources, influenced the freedom of executive leaders to exercise their own will. Donaldson and Lorsch (1983) argued that one of the prime determinants of CEOs' focus on financial performance was their psychological need for autonomy. Quite simply, the better their firms perform, the less scrutiny and

Exhibit 2.2 Industry Context Sorted by Industry Profitability

Standard Industrial Classification	Industry Name	Industry Return on Assets
5331	Variety stores	.063
8744	Facilities support services	.063
8741	Management services	.062
8011	Offices/medical clinics	.061
5411	Grocery stores	.061
5399	Miscellaneous general merchandise stores	.054
7832	Motion picture theaters	.049
7011	Hotels and motels	.048
5013	Motor vehicle supplies	.048
6712	Bank holding companies	.046
2253	Knit outerwear mills	.040
3567	Industrial furnaces/ovens	.043
5159	Farm-product raw materials	.040
8051	Skilled nursing care	.040
4924	Natural gas production	.039
4512	Air transportation	.038
2873	Nitrogeneous fertilizers	.038
5141	Groceries	.037
8063	Psychiatric hospitals	.036
6512	Nonresidential building operations	.034
2824	Organic fibers	.034
4911	Electric services	.033
5311	Department stores	.031
8069	Specialty hospitals	.030
1311	Crude petroleum and natural gas	.027
6162	Mortgage bankers	.009

second-guessing CEOs get from board members, shareholders, customers, and employees. Therefore, it is helpful to know something about the financial standing or slack resources of the organizations in which these CEOs operate.

Furthermore, the corporate strategy, or level of firm diversification, has been found to influence managerial discretion. For example, Napier and Smith (1987) found that the proportion of a corporate manager's incentive pay was significantly greater in more diversified (and hence, higher discretion) firms, and Michel and Hambrick (1992) discovered that the firm's diversification posture was systematically related to the characteristics of the firm's top executives. These studies suggest that

Exhibit 2.3 Organizational Characteristics for Responding CEOs

Organizational Characteristic	Low	High	Mean	Median
Size:				
Number of employees	2	64,840	3,640	554
Sales ($ thousands)	18	8,210,884	533,940	75,858
Assets ($ thousands)	83	1,715,000	804,602	162,463
Market value ($ millions)	$7.9	$5,255.7	$636.9	$158.3
Board control:				
Number of inside directors	1	8	2.4	2
Board size	1	26	8.0	7
Financial standing:				
Return on assets	−264%	27%	−4.0%	3.0%
Three-year sales growth	−43.3	1255.7	38.3	14.5
Price-earnings ratio	−650	158.3	6.2	13.7
Product-market diversity[a]	1	6	2.0	2

NOTE: All data are for 1996.
a. Calculated as the number of four-digit SIC codes.

the level of firm diversification influences managerial discretion as well. In sum, organizational size, board of director characteristics, slack resources, and the corporate strategy have all been shown to be important contextual factors surrounding strategic leaders.

We begin our examination of organizational context by first examining the sizes of organizations represented in this study. Notably, a wide variety of organizational sizes were represented in our sample. As shown in Exhibit 2.3, the average responding firm had 3,640 employees, with over $500,000 in revenues, more than $800,000 in assets, and $637 million in market value. However, there was a considerable range of sizes represented in this sample. For example, the smallest firm had only $7.9 million in market value whereas the largest firm had over $5.2 billion in market value. This range in size suggests that there is considerable variation in organizational size and, therefore, context represented in our sample.

Previous research suggests that it is also useful to examine the financial standing, or slack resources, of the responding firms. Exhibit 2.3 shows that the median return on assets (ROA) was 3.0%, but ROAs ranged from a high of 27% to a low of −264%. In addition, the 3-year annual sales growth for this sample averaged 38.3%; but it ranged from −43% to more than 1000% per year, and the price-earnings (P/E) ratios averaged 6.2, but ranged from a P/E of −650 to a high of 158. Clearly, there are varying degrees of financial strength represented in this sample, which suggests variation in opportunities for executive discretion.

As mentioned previously, research has shown that when the proportion of insiders is relatively high, the board is relatively large, and the CEO also chairs the board, the CEO has considerable discretion. Exhibit 2.3 also provides information indicating the level of board control surrounding the CEOs in this study. The CEOs were members of governing boards that ranged in size from 1 to 26 people with a median membership of 7. In 44% of those boards, the CEO was also the chairman. The number of insiders ranged from 1 to 8 people, with a median membership of 2 inside directors.

In some firms, the CEO is firmly in control. For example, Back Yard Burgers, Inc., has a seven-person board with four insiders and the CEO as chairman. Clearly, the CEO of this firm has quite a bit of discretion with this board. In contrast, Martin Marietta Materials also has a seven-person board, but the only insider on it is the CEO, and an outside director chairs the board. In this situation, the CEO has less direct control of the board. In sum, there is considerable variation in CEO discretion with respect to the board of directors.

Finally, the corporate strategies, or levels of diversification, pursued by the responding firms are also documented in Exhibit 2.3. Diversification was operationalized as the number of industries in which the firm generated sales in 1996. This product-count approach revealed the median number of industries in which the firm was active was 2, but the industry count ranged from 1 (a nondiversified single business) to 6 (a relatively diversified conglomerate).

Demographic Characteristics of CEOs

Executive leadership and discretion are not automatically determined by the environmental and organizational context. Executives also influence and change their organizations (Finkelstein & Hambrick, 1996) and environments (Norburn, 1986). One set of variables that have been found to be predictive of some executive actions is their demographic characteristics. These characteristics are easily observable external personal descriptors that include such things as gender, age, tenure, and compensation.

CEO Gender

Women have made enormous inroads into the management ranks of U.S. industry. For example, women constitute nearly half of the U.S. labor force and a growing proportion of entry-level and middle-level management positions. Furthermore, women held 17% of the managerial positions in 1972, and this proportion had grown to 42.7% in 1995 (Ragins, Townsend, & Mattis, 1998).

Despite this rising tide of female managers, less than 5% of senior management positions in major U.S. corporations are held by women (Baum, 1987; Lawler, 1994; Loden, 1987). Furthermore, *Fortune* magazine recently reported that less than 0.5% of the highest paid officers and directors of corporations were women (Fierman, 1990). In light of these facts, it is not surprising that it is relatively uncommon to find women in the CEO's position. This fact is especially true for large organizations: No woman currently occupies the CEO post in any of the *Fortune* 500 firms (Townsend, 1996), and there are only three female CEOs in the largest 1,000 firms in the United States (Cleland, 1994).

However, women are increasingly assuming the role of CEO in small and medium-size firms. Evidently, a growing number of successful female business executives are leaving large corporations and starting their own firms out of frustration with rigid, hierarchical, and male-dominated cultures (Lawler, 1994). The Small Business Administration reports that businesses owned by women now account for the fastest-growing part of the U.S. economy (Machan, 1989). This trend has caused some researchers to recommend further research and analysis on how this fundamental difference manifests itself in the chief executive role (Finkelstein & Hambrick, 1996, p. 106).

Consistent with common practice and the research literature, all of the 416 CEOs surveyed were male; hence, all 91 survey respondents were male. Clearly, it is a rare event to have a woman in the CEO position in a publicly held corporation. In sum, our sample is representative of the larger population of CEOs, which has few, if any, women among its ranks.[1]

CEO Age

Relatively little is known about how the CEO's age affects his role as chief executive, other than the common observation and prediction

Exhibit 2.4 Demographic Characteristics of Responding CEOs

CEO Characteristic	Low	High	Mean	Median
Age	30	77	53.4	54
Organizational tenure	1	56	15.1	12
Job tenure	1	42	9.3	7
Compensation	$44,785	$2,348,296	$431,551.0	$287,762

NOTE: All data are for 1996.

that older CEOs are expected to be more risk averse than younger CEOs (Finkelstein & Hambrick, 1996). We do know, however, that the median age of CEOs is increasing in the 20th century, starting at 53 years in 1900 and increasing to 58 years in 1989 (Kurtz, Boone, & Fleenor, 1989). Some research has found that, holding all other variables constant, CEO age is inversely related to firm financial performance (Finley & Buntzman, 1994). Other research has found that CEO age has a curvilinear relationship with the likelihood of takeover resistance (Buchholtz & Ribbens, 1994). Furthermore, Levinson (1978) argues that men in their 50s and 60s approach life in very different ways than men in their 30s and 40s. In sum, the age of the CEO is likely to have a significant impact on their leadership behavior.

The CEOs in this study averaged 53.4 years old. The youngest CEO in this study was 30, and the oldest was 77, with a median age of 54 (refer to Exhibit 2.4). Overall, the respondents to our study are distributed similarly to national averages, but slightly younger than the national averages. Coincident with this similarity to the general population of CEOs, there was quite a wide range of ages represented in our research study.

CEO Tenure

CEO tenure refers to the number of years the CEO has occupied the role as chief executive for the firm. In the past, most CEO turnover occurred due to retirement. However, in the 1990s, shortened tenures and involuntary turnover are becoming increasingly the norm. For example, experts now estimate that CEO tenure has decreased from roughly 10 years in the 1980s to 7 years in the 1990s. Those same experts predict that CEO tenure will continue to decline (Grube, 1995). A major cause of these shortened tenures is the rise of institutional activism and increasingly vigilant outside directors.

Previous research on CEO tenure has shown that it has a predictable sequence of seasons (Hambrick & Fukotomi, 1991). Overall, the researchers argued that in the first 2 years of the CEO's job, he often demonstrates flexibility and usually avoids major commitments as he learns about the nature of the job. This often is a period of great experimentation, and the central focus is the selection of an enduring theme. In years three to five, the CEO begins to close off options, make conclusions from the early experiments, and aim all actions at bolstering the chosen theme. In years six and beyond, the typical CEO has extreme filters on incoming information, outside interests often increase, and the established paradigm or status quo is vigorously protected and defended.

Unfortunately, not much research exists to test these ideas, but there are a few exceptions. Recent research shows that the more outside directors are aware of the CEO's decision-making style, the shorter the CEO's tenure (Judge & Dobbins, 1995). Similarly, other research found that the board's ability to link the CEO's compensation to organizational performance decreases over time as the CEO's tenure increases (Hill & Phan, 1991). Also, Miller (1991) found that CEOs tended to become "stale in the saddle" as their tenure increased, but organizations were less able to challenge this staleness over time. Overall, we know that CEOs' tenures are decreasing in general, but the CEO's power increases as his tenure on the job increases.

As can be seen in Exhibit 2.4, the average respondent in this study had been employed by his organization for 15 years and had served in the CEO position for 9 of those 15 years. One early tenure CEO was new to the organization; at the other extreme, another "well seasoned" CEO had been the chief executive officer of his firm for 42 years and had worked within that same firm for more than 56 years.

CEO Compensation

Perhaps no other demographic variable in the executive suite has received as much media and research attention as CEO compensation. We know, for example, that CEO compensation continues to rise to very high levels, often independent of the company's performance level or other employee compensation and employment trends. For example, the after-tax real wage of the average worker in the United States has fallen in the last 20 years, whereas the average CEO has received infla-tion-adjusted pay raises of over 300% (Tevlin, 1996). Continuing this trend, total compensation for CEOs grew 30% from 1995 to 1996, but most employees' wages remained stagnant (Pratt, 1996). With stock options omitted, the median total annual CEO compensation in the largest U.S. companies is roughly $1.5 million, according to a Towers Perrin annual study (Pratt, 1996).

Some observers argue that the problem is not so much the high levels of CEO compensation, but the tenuous relationship between CEO compensation and the company's performance. For example, two fi-nance experts recently reported that CEO compensation declines by a small amount when a firm's bond rating is downgraded; however, CEO compensation increases dramatically when the bond rating is upgraded (Fosberg & James, 1995). Similarly, recent management research dem-onstrated that the CEO's power was much more predictive of his com-pensation than the firm's performance levels (Boyd, 1994; Sanders, Davis-Blake, & Fredrickson, 1995). In sum, the high and dramatic growth of CEO compensation, coupled with the lack of employee wage increases and absence of a systematic relation between CEO compen-sation and firm performance, assures that this topic will be of great interest to society for years to come.

Ignoring stock options and deferred compensation, the average salary earned by the CEOs in this study was more than $431,000 per year. Their salaries ranged from a low of $44,000 to a high of $2.35 million per year. This is considerably lower than the $1.5 million figure quoted above because it is derived from smaller firms, and we know that the size of the firm is highly correlated with the compensation provided. Despite this lower level of compensation compared to the largest firms in the United States, this is clearly a well-compensated and affluent group of individuals.

Case Studies of Contexts
Surrounding Seven CEOs

Let us continue with introductions and description of the contextual situation confronting the seven CEOs whose lives we will follow throughout this book. The seven pseudonyms are: Robert Masters, Michael Breen, Joseph Henderson, Richard Farr, Raymond Zucker-man, Randy Maxwell, and Steven Zolte.

Robert Masters

Robert joined his company as a sales manager in 1967. The company was developing new technologies to burn environmentally hazardous waste material, but sales were slow initially due to the lack of environmental standards. In 1970, some national standards were established with the passage of the Clean Air Act by Congress, and states and municipalities followed these standards closely. As a result, the company grew quickly.

Along with this growth came new opportunities, and Robert handled them well. He was promoted to vice president of sales in 1973, corporate secretary in 1977, and then executive vice president in 1979. In 1985, Robert was promoted to CEO of this company, and all looked rosy. Robert was 55 years old at that time, and the company was experiencing steady and consistent growth in sales and profitability.

However, the company's sales manager was not content. He passionately believed the company could grow much faster and pitched this idea to Robert. Robert listened to his proposal but considered it to be too risky and declined to pursue it further. This response frustrated the 32-year-old sales manager, and he resolved to push his ideas further with the company's major stockholder. In 1990, the sales manager privately approached this majority stockholder and convinced him to try out some new technologies and market opportunities. Indeed, this major stockholder was so sold on this proposal that he promoted the sales manager to the CEO position and demoted Robert to his former executive vice president position in February 1991.

Surprised and dejected with this sudden turn of events, Robert recalls, "I came very close to leaving, and to this day I don't know why I did not leave. But I stayed." The new CEO pushed the company into the new markets, and sales grew from $14 million in 1990 to $27 million in 1991. However, the company lost $2.7 million—its first red ink in the company's history. Furious with this turn of events and not trusting the new CEO, valuable top managers left the company. Long-standing customers began to be neglected, and several board members quit. The company moved perilously close to bankruptcy.

By June 1992, the new CEO was fired, and a new board of directors was assembled. After their first meeting, they approached Robert and asked him to return as CEO. According to Robert, "I think that they thought I would jump at it, but I didn't. I took a while to think it over and then accepted the position after I got some things clear within me and with them."

When asked why he accepted the job, Robert replied,

> I don't know for sure. We had 312 employees at our high point, and by the time I took the job a second time, we were down to 50. I had to cut employment down to 30 at one point to save the company, and that really hurt. Some of those people had been around almost as long as I had. My goal was to preserve the nucleus of the company—especially folks in engineering and manufacturing. Also, I felt some responsibility to those folks because I had hired a lot of them myself. Getting rid of someone because they deserve it is one thing, but downsizing folks when they are doing a good job is a totally different situation. It was the toughest period of my life. I never want to go through that again.

In 1996, the company was back to its steady growth again with 40 employees. Robert was 61 years old, and he was paid an annual salary of $112,500. He chaired the board of directors, and three outside directors sat on this board with him. The company's profitability was slightly above the industry average of 4.4% return on assets. Battle-scarred, but not beaten, Robert looked to the future.

Michael Breen

Michael had spent the lion's share of his career working for a large national bank. He was very productive and achieved steady promotions to higher and higher levels of responsibility. Then one day, a headhunter contacted him and offered him the presidency of a small bank located in the Southeast. Michael's response was, "No, I don't want to leave. I have been here too long. I'm too comfortable. They've been too good to me, and I'm too loyal. Thanks for thinking of me, but I am not interested." They chatted a bit further and then ended the conversation amicably.

Undeterred, the headhunter called back 2 weeks later. He maintained that this job was really a perfect fit between Michael's skills and interests and the bank's needs and convinced him to meet at a local airport to discuss the matter further. Michael reasoned that he really had little to lose; so he met with the headhunter, visited the bank 2 weeks later, and assumed the CEO's position 2 weeks after that. At age 42, Michael felt like an entrepreneur.

In 1996, Michael had been CEO for 2 years and was paid a $274,000 salary. The company has grown 30% per year under his direction and is quickly moving to be a top performer among the regional banks in the United States. With 485 employees and over $80 million in annual revenues, the company was recently listed by several Wall Street firms with strong "buy" recommendations. Internally, Michael chaired all board meetings, but he was the only insider among the 11-member board of directors. The decision to assume the CEO's role looked like a smart decision for Michael, as he was enjoying the responsibility, and the results were encouraging.

Joseph Henderson

Joseph had risen in the ranks of a large, health care-delivery firm. As he studied the health care industry, he increasingly sensed that the industry was about to go through tremendous change. So he increasingly became concerned about the firm's future. In his own words,

> I kind of gravitated to the role of the person that would say in meetings, "Change is coming. We need to face it." It was not a very popular position to take because the company was doing so well. So the conclusion on the part of the rest of top management was: "Well if you are so convinced things are going to change, why don't you take all the areas that will confront this change." And so I ended up taking all the new ventures.

One of the new ventures was a multibillion-dollar joint venture with an insurance firm. It was initially very successful, and Joseph was the representative for his firm in maintaining the relationship and guiding the venture. However, after about a year, "the thing became totally political" to use Joseph's words. Although the venture was hitting its financial targets, the two partners began to develop different views of it. As their differences grew, things came to a head, with one partner wanting to move faster and another partner wanting to slow things down. Eventually, relations deteriorated to such an extent that the joint venture was dissolved and representatives from both firms were fired. At 45 years old, Joseph was without a job for the first time in his adult life.

After this turn of events, Joseph expected to rejoin some other established firm in the health care industry, as that was his primary base of expertise. However, his entrepreneurial instincts stayed with him, and he had an idea for a new health care-services firm in 1986 that would tackle health care costs without compromising quality. He was convinced that the idea could work in the changing industry, but he was reluctant to start a new firm at the age of 45. However, the idea kept bubbling up inside of him; and ultimately, he concluded that "This is what you need to do."

So he approached three other individuals whom he respected and explained the concept to them. They immediately agreed to join him in the new venture. Next, they pulled together a business plan and got $3 million of venture capital funding from the first firm they approached. Shortly after that, they raised another $3 million and then another $18 million. One year later, they took the firm public at about $16 a share.

In 1996, Joseph earned an annual salary of $550,000 in his sixth year as CEO. His organization employed over 5,300 employees and earned over $440 million in revenues. Furthermore, his firm consistently beat the average profitability of its competitors, despite the fact that industry profitability was growing nearly 10% a year. Perhaps, this is why the company's stock was currently trading at $115 to $120 a share (a P/E ratio of 52). In addition to being CEO, Joseph also served as chairman for the board meetings. The board comprised 10 members, 4 insiders and 6 outsiders. At 54 years old, Joseph looked forward to a bright future.

Richard Farr

Richard worked in the banking industry all his life. He started in high school. His mother worked in a small local bank, and when he didn't have anything to do, he would visit her and "hang out" at the bank. During one particular visit, he was asked to photograph checks one at a time, and he immediately performed that task. As often happens, that led to a part-time job. After college and graduate school, he went right back into banking and joined a large bank. That worked well for a while, but he eventually started getting bored with the bureaucracy and rules and started looking around him. He saw that banking wasn't

as progressive as it could be, so he got the idea of starting a data-processing service for the banking industry. In so doing, he started dealing
with community banks that needed his data-processing expertise. This
was going well for a while, and then he took some time to sit back and
reflect. Richard states,

> I became intrigued because community banking is a lot differ-
> ent from big banking, and its fun. After one trip to a community
> bank, I sat down with a close friend and said, "You know what
> we really ought to do, instead of working our fanny to death
> creating a service bureau? We ought to go and found a bank!"
> We started thinking and talking and, you know, it's one of those
> things where you have an idea and all of a sudden, you really
> fall in love with it. And we kept talking and then assembled a
> group of managers, and we had everything, but one thing. We
> didn't have any money!

In September 1988, Richard came across the path of Gordon Dietz,
"a man who had the same vision and values" as himself. Gordon had
started a bank 20 years earlier in another part of the state and was quite
successful. Richard and Gordon kept talking to each other over a period
of 2 to 3 months to make sure their styles were compatible and their
visions were aligned. Over the course of these talks, Gordon became
like a surrogate father to Richard; and they eventually agreed to work
together—Gordon provided the capital and local market knowledge,
and Richard provided the management expertise and eye for innovation, which "a lot of bankers don't have."

In December 1989, 1 year after Richard and Gordon agreed to work
together, the new bank was opened with an initial capitalization of $6
million. Half of the money came from Gordon, and the other half came
from 350 other investors, many of whom were prospective customers
of the bank. The bank has grown its asset and customer base in the
ensuing years.

In 1996, 5 years into the role of CEO, Richard earned a salary of
$106,000. He was one of two insiders who sat on the six-person board,
but Gordon (an outside director and major stockholder) chaired all
board meetings. The bank employed 23 people and achieved $4 million
in revenues that year. Growth was limited in sales and profitability, but
the bank was hitting its financial targets. At age 47, Richard was optimistic about his future and the future of the bank.

Raymond Zuckerman

Raymond's parents owned a small "dime" store when he was born in 1934. His parents had a gift for retailing, and the family business grew dramatically in the 1930s and 1940s. Of course, Raymond worked in the family business during the summers and after school. In 1953, Raymond went off to the Korean War and, when he returned in 1956, he decided that he wanted to rejoin the family business. At the time, his cousin was partnering with his father; but his cousin wanted out. So he bought his cousin's share of the business, and he and his father launched a new retailing enterprise in 1960.

In 1996, Raymond earned an annual salary of $784,000 at the age of 62, following 12 years as CEO and 30 years as a company employee. His firm employed more than 50,000 employees throughout the United States, and it commanded over $4 billion in annual revenues. Raymond also served as chairman for the seven-person board, of which five were outsiders and two were insiders—Raymond and his chief financial officer. However, the firm was only marginally profitable, and its P/E ratio was under 10. As a result, Raymond was giving serious thought to replacing several members of his top management team and restructuring the entire organization.

Randy Maxwell

Randy was born and raised on a farm in Kansas. He graduated from high school and went to Vietnam as a helicopter pilot. After returning from Vietnam, Randy went to college and joined an international chemical company as a sales representative in their crop chemicals division. He spent 10 years in both sales and marketing positions while at this firm. The last job he had at this company was as marketing manager for Japan and Taiwan. He was stationed in Tokyo and loved his work, but he was ambitious and soon found new opportunities.

Randy then joined another multinational chemical company and spent 5 years there—3 years as the vice president of their international animal health business. In that position, he increasingly had differences with his boss. In Randy's words,

> I got crossways with a rather unpleasant boss. There were clear differences in terms of strategy, philosophy, and even ethics. I

liked the company a lot, but this boss had some real problems, so I started looking for other opportunities.

With the aid of a corporate headhunter, he was asked to assume the CEO position of a new, biotechnology company with potential international markets in animal health. Although he had never planned to become a CEO, he accepted the position, as it was "an exciting challenge and kept me in the international marketing arena."

When he joined this company in January 1990, the company was little more than some venture capital and a concept, with 26 employees sharing a dream. The firm had $15,000 of revenues and a $7 million loss in his first year as CEO. In the 1990s, Randy has provided guidance to the research and development efforts; established subsidiaries in Europe, the Middle East, and Africa; and successfully navigated the firm through the ups and downs of the biotechnology industry.

In 1996, Randy earned a salary of $160,000 as CEO. The firm had 114 full-time employees and achieved $14 million in annual revenues. Being in the biotechnology industry with heavy product-development efforts, the firm had not yet earned a profit. Randy sat on the board of directors, but he was the only insider among the six-person board; and he did not chair the board. At age 47 and with 6 years under his belt as CEO, Randy was bullish about the future.

Steven Zolte

Steven graduated from college, got married, and then went to work for a year or so. To fulfill a military obligation, he joined the U.S. Army and served in Vietnam for 3.5 years, disarming live explosives. When he came out of the military at age 29, he immediately earned a master's degree in behavioral science to complement his technical training and went to work training police officers how to disarm bombs. Commenting on this experience, he stated,

Working with explosives was really good experience for me. One of the questions you get asked as a public company CEO is, "How do you cope with the pressure of quarterly earnings?" And I just look at the guy and say, "I used to disarm bombs for a living. You really don't understand what real pressure is."

Next, Steven went to work at a construction materials company that was eventually sold to a large conglomerate. During that time, he earned an MBA in the evenings and concluded that he wanted to be the CEO of a billion-dollar public company before he finished his business career. Steven was the general manager of a large operating unit within this conglomerate in 1982 and well on his way to fulfilling his ambitious dream. In the early 1990s, a large diversified firm acquired his multidivisional company; and his unit was spun off in 1994 due to lack of "strategic fit." Steven kept his top management team intact and became the CEO of a public firm during that same year. He was well on his way to completing his dream if he could just grow the business.

In 1996, Steven earned a salary over $500,000 and was the only insider on the seven-person board of directors. His firm employed more than 4,000 workers, exceeded $600 million in revenues, and earned a 9% return on assets in 1996. At 50 years of age, Steven was well on his way toward achieving his dream of being a CEO of a billion-dollar publicly held firm.

Summing Up

Context matters. The organizational and environmental context influences executive opportunities and discretion and mind-set. These background conditions set the stage on which executive leaders shine their lights or cast their shadows.

Overall, the CEOs in this study are confronted with a wide range of contexts within which they exercise strategic leadership. Some key variations in the organizational context include the following:

- Fifty-seven different industries were represented in this study, with no industry representing more than 5% of the sample other than the banking industry.
- Firms ranged in size from 2 to 65,000 employees.
- Some firms were losing money badly while others were making record profits.
- Some boards of directors were fairly independent of the CEO whereas others were under the CEO's control.
- Some firms were in a single line of business whereas others were highly diversified.

In addition to all this variation in the organizational context, there was considerable variation in the demographic profiles of the CEOs. For example, CEOs varied on the following dimensions:

- CEO ages ranged from 30 to 77 years old.
- Some CEOs were new to the job and the organization, whereas others had decades of industry and organizational experience.
- CEO salaries ranged from as little as $44,000 to a high of $2.3 million.

As the seven case studies suggest, context "illuminates" different facets of the leader's character; and it serves as a screen on which the shadow is cast. Although it is necessary to know the context in which leadership takes place, that context does not determine how leadership unfolds, nor does it strictly limit the possibilities for the future. That dynamic is a function of the leader's character, which is the central focus and primary contribution of this book.

Individual Shadow Work With Context

1. What surprises you about the backgrounds of the seven CEO case studies? Which case study interested you most? Why? What can you learn from their backgrounds and contexts?
2. It has been said that there are two basic paths of change—reacting to a crisis or proactively seeking a new order. Which is more common? Why is that so?
3. Write your personal biography. Focus on the milestones but examine the turning points carefully. What are the contextual influences on your life? Who and what have had a major influence on your life? What qualities have emerged in you as a result of those influences?

PART II

Character of Executive Leaders

3

Personalities of Executive Leaders

Many young people today are afraid to grow up because the adults they see look bored, depressed, or preoccupied by heavy responsibilities.

— Judith Provost, 1990, p. 83

The psyche is still a foreign, almost unexplored country of which we have only indirect knowledge; it is mediated by conscious functions that are subject to almost endless possibilities of deception.

— Carl Jung, 1933, p. 75

The one thing that our unconscious will not tolerate is evasion of responsibility. The unconscious pushes us into one suffering after another, one impossible mess after another, until we are finally willing to wake up, see that it is we who are choosing these impossible paths, and take responsibility for our own decisions.

— Robert Johnson, 1986, p. 93

How can I be substantial if I fail to cast a shadow? I must have a dark side also if I am to be whole; and inasmuch as I become conscious of my shadow I also remember that I am a human being like any other.

— Carl Jung, 1933, p. 35

There is increasing evidence suggesting that executive personality matters. For example, we know that personality traits influence how the CEO manages his top management team and the rest of the organization

(Miller & Toulouse, 1986a; Nahavandi, Malezadeh, & Mizzi, 1991). Similarly, we know that the CEOs who are impatient, impulsive, manipulative, dominating, self-important, and overly critical are more likely to fail than other CEOs (Grant, 1996). Furthermore, certain CEO personality traits have even been found to be associated with higher levels of firm performance (Miller & Toulouse, 1986b). As a result, we begin our exploration of executive leaders' character by examining their personalities.

There are many conceptualizations of personality, but one of the most powerful and popular frameworks comes from the famous Swiss psychologist, Carl Jung. According to Jung (1923), personality reflects both our conscious and unconscious minds. The conscious mind is what we are aware of regarding ourselves; the unconscious mind is what we are not aware of regarding ourselves. From his extensive clinical practice, he concluded that there are a limited number of personality types and that each individual is born with a preference for a certain type. He argued that each of these personality types is equally valuable, but our environment (e.g., parents, teachers, religious leaders, friends) either encourages or discourages the expression of our inborn personality type.

A second reason Jung's theory of personality is so pertinent to this book is because he takes a developmental perspective and offers important ideas about a person's shadow. Jung believed that our personalities are dynamic over our lives: The first half of life should be dedicated to embracing our inborn personality types, and the second half of life should be dedicated to embracing the polar opposites of our inborn types, or our "shadow" personality (Corlett & Millner, 1993).

According to Jung, the shadow is like a foreign personality, a primitive, instinctual kind of being. It is everything we do not want others to know about us and everything we don't even want to know about ourselves. The recognition of the shadow, or moving the shadow from our unconscious into our conscious, requires considerable moral courage and much effort. Robert Bly (1988) likened our relationship with our shadow personality to a bag slung over our shoulder—out of reach and out of sight, we lug it throughout our lives with all the aspects of ourselves that are rejected by others and by ourselves.

But before we explore our shadow or "less preferred" self, we must first identify what our personality, or "preferred" self, is. One of the most popular methods of assessing personality is the Myers-Briggs Type

Exhibit 3.1 Personality Type Distribution of the U.S. Adult Population

ISTJ	ISFJ	INFJ	INTJ	Dichotomous Preferences:
n = 198	n = 146	n = 33	n = 44	Extrovert n = 587 (46.3%)
(15.6%)	(11.5%)	(2.6%)	(3.5%)	Introvert n = 680 (53.7%)
++++++ ++++++ +++	++++++ ++++++	+++	++++	Sensor n = 863 (68.1%) iNtuitive n = 404 (31.9%) Thinking n = 670 (52.9%) Feeling n = 597 (47.1%)
ISTP n = 81 (6.4%) ++++++	**ISFP** n = 57 (4.5%) +++++	**INFP** n = 55 (4.3%) ++++	**INTP** n = 66 (5.2%) +++++	Judging n = 736 (58.1%) Perceiving n = 531 (41.9%) Pairs and Temperaments:
ESTP n = 61 (4.8%) +++++	**ESFP** n = 72 (5.7%) ++++++	**ENFP** n = 80 (6.3%) ++++++	**ENTP** n = 59 (4.7%) +++++	IJ n = 421 (32.2%) IP n = 259 (20.4%) EP n = 272 (24.9%) EJ n = 315 (24.9%) ST n = 466 (36.8%) SF n = 397 (31.3%) NF n = 200 (15.8%) NT n = 204 (16.1%) SJ n = 592 (46.7%) SP n = 271 (21.4%) NP n = 260 (20.5%)
ESTJ n = 126 (9.9%) ++++++ ++++	**ESFJ** n = 122 (9.6%) ++++++ ++++	**ENFJ** n = 32 (2.5%) +++	**ENTJ** n = 35 (2.8%) +++	NJ n = 144 (11.4%) TJ n = 403 (31.8%) TP n = 267 (21.1%) FP n = 264 (20.8%) FJ n = 333 (26.3%) IN n = 198 (15.6%) EN n = 206 (16.3%) IS n = 482 (38.0%) ES n = 381 (30.1%)

SOURCE: Hammer & Mitchell, 1996. Reprinted by permission.
NOTE: N = 1,267; + = 1% of N.

Indicator (MBTI) (Myers & McCaulley, 1993). Over 3 million Americans take the MBTI each year, and it now has been translated into 12 foreign languages (Gardner & Martinko, 1996). Moreover, the use of the MBTI is likely to increase as organizations use it for such diverse purposes as management education, organizational development, career counseling, team building, and even decision making (Walck, 1992).

Exhibit 3.1 has the personality-type preferences for the American adult population. It is provided as a basis of comparison to the CEO population in this study. As you can see, there are 16 different personality types in this framework; Americans can be found in all types, although some are more common than others. The remaining discussion will explore what these types are and how CEOs in our research study compared to the American population.

Personality Characteristics of CEOs

Mitroff (1983) was one of the first management researchers to suggest that the manager's personality preferences were intimately linked to the manager's perceptions and behavior. Interestingly, Mitroff argued that the manager's personality could be construed as an inner social system that guides a manager's assumptions about external stakeholders. Furthermore, Mitroff reasoned that just as external stakeholder needs can conflict with organizational interests, inner personality drives can conflict with organizational interests.

Mitroff was highly influenced and attracted to the ideas of Carl Jung. Unlike most personality theorists, Jung posited that individual personalities differed by discrete categories of personality types rather than along a continuum of personality traits. Jung argued that each individual was born with a preference for one pole along each of these personality dimensions, and recent research has documented this assertion in the general population (Quenk, 1993), as well as with CEOs (Rytting, Ware, & Prince, 1994). Each of Jung's four personality dimensions (i.e., energy source, data collection, decision making, and lifestyle orientation) will be discussed in greater depth below, as each offers interesting new insights into the CEO's inner character.

Personality Preference No. 1: Energy Source

The executive leader's job is very demanding and requires much energy. The typical executive leader must scan an increasingly complex and discontinuous environment, interpret the literally millions of signals derived from that scan, and often mobilize thousands of employees to change. Clearly, the executive doesn't do all this by himself; however, the fact that he must address this chaos through dozens of people makes the job that much more demanding. In sum, executive leaders must have a relatively high level of energy to reach their position as well as to continue performing adequately.

Jung noted that there are two ways by which individuals gain or lose energy. One way of gaining energy is through external stimuli by engaging a wide variety of tasks, people, and/or things. This energy source preference is known as the *Extroverted* approach. In contrast, some individuals gain energy by going within by limiting external stimuli and focusing on inner thoughts and feelings. This preference is known as the *Introverted* approach.

These two personality preferences are seen as complementary and functional attitudes toward life. In the extroverted attitude, attention seems to flow out, or to be drawn out, to the objects and people of the environment. The main interests of the extrovert are the outer world of people and things. In contrast, the introverted attitude experiences energy being drawn from the environment and consolidated within one's position. The main interests of the introvert are with the inner world of concepts and ideas (Myers & McCaulley, 1993).

Based on previous research, we know the American public shows a slight preference for introversion, with roughly 54% of Americans scoring as introverts and 46% scoring as extroverts (Hammer & Mitchell, 1996). Unfortunately, previous management research has largely ignored this dimension of personality (Walck, 1992). What we do know, however, is that CEOs are more likely to be extroverted in nature (Roach, 1982). For example, Pollitt (1982) reported that 66% of the CEOs/general managers that he worked with in his 10 years of consulting were extroverted in nature. Similarly, Reynierse (1993) reported that 60% of senior executives and CEOs were extroverts.

In my research study of CEOs, the overwhelming majority of our respondents were shown to be extroverted in nature (71%); the remainder were shown to be introverted in nature (29%). This finding is consistent with previous research, which has found that the CEO position attracts extroverts. CEOs' work involves a wide variety of people and tasks—people who are extroverted may be drawn to and/or excel in this type of work environment.

Personality Preference No. 2: Data Collection

Jung divided all perceptive or data-collecting activities into two categories—*Sensing* and *iNtuition*. The sensing preference refers to data collected by way of the five senses. It is oriented to the here and now experiences in the present moment. The sensing preference seeks the fullest possible experience of what is immediate and real. In contrast, the intuitive preference refers to the perception of possibilities, meanings, and relationships by way of insight. Intuition permits data collection beyond what is accessible to the senses, including possible future events. Also, it seeks the furthest reaches of the possible and imaginative (Myers & McCaulley, 1993). In the American adult population, the vast majority have a preference for the sensing approach (68.1%).

In my research study of CEOs, the predominant type was the intuitive preference (63%); less common was the sensing preference (37%). Clearly, this is in stark contrast to the general American population, which is highly sensing oriented. Previous management research has shown that executives oriented toward the sensing preference are more likely to use standardized procedures and focus on details as compared to relatively intuitive executives, who are more likely to use new methods and focus on the "big picture" (Hellriegel & Slocum, 1980; Reynierse, 1993; Roach, 1982).

Personality Preference No. 3: Decision Making

The third dimension of personality that Jung proposed is the judgment or decision-making preference. Decision making is the process of coming to a conclusion about what has been perceived. As before, Jung argued that there are two ways of making decisions—the *Thinking* preference and the *Feeling* preference. Those who prefer thinking seek rational order and plan according to systematic logic. People who are primarily oriented toward thinking value highly objectivity and logic. In contrast, those who prefer feeling seek rational order according to harmony among subjective values. These people often have a concern for the human aspects of problems rather than the technical aspects (Myers & McCaulley, 1993). In the American adult population, the proportion of thinkers (52.9%) is roughly equivalent to the proportion of feelers (47.1%).

Unlike the general population, the CEOs in our study were primarily given to the thinking preference. In fact, three fourths of our sample demonstrated this preference, whereas only one fourth showed a preference for the feeling orientation. Previous management research has repeatedly shown that people with the thinking preference value cool, impersonal logic, whereas those with the feeling preference value harmony much more highly (Hellriegel & Slocum, 1980; Mitroff & Kilmann, 1975; Roach, 1982; Taggert & Robey, 1981). Furthermore, research has shown that managers with the thinking preference often rely solely on quantitative analysis whereas managers with the feeling preference are more comfortable with qualitative analysis (Mitroff, Barabba, & Kilmann, 1977).

Personality Preference No. 4: Lifestyle Orientation

Jung described the Extroversion-Introversion, Sensing-iNtuition, and Thinking-Feeling preferences explicitly in his work; the orientation to the outer world or lifestyle orientation was only implicit in Jung's work. It was made explicit by Isabell Myers and Katharine Briggs in their attempt to operationalize Jung's concepts. As before, there are two preferences for this dimension, *Perceiving* and *Judging* types. When a person prefers the perceiving orientation, that person is attuned to incoming information and is open, curious, and spontaneous. In contrast, when a person prefers the judging orientation, that person is concerned with making decisions, seeking closure, planning operations, or organizing activities (Myers & McCaulley, 1993). In the general population, a majority (58.1%) lean toward the judging orientation, whereas a minority (41.9%) are inclined toward the perceiving orientation.

To an even greater degree than the general population, our CEOs demonstrated a preference for the judging orientation. In fact, exactly two thirds (67%) showed a judging orientation, and one third (33%) showed a perceiving orientation. Unfortunately, there isn't much empirical research on the lifestyle orientation of executives other than the disproportionate preference for the judging orientation over the perceiving orientation in the executive suite (Walck, 1992).

Overall Personality Preferences

The overall distribution of CEOs' personality preferences in our research study is listed in Exhibit 3.2. This table provides summary statistics of the 16 personality types, as well as statistics on various combinations of these four personality dimensions. Whereas 11 of the 16 personality types are represented by our research sample, it is clear that the CEO's role is most often filled by people with the NT type personality, especially the ENTJ type.

The four mental functions (i.e., Sensing, iNtuition, Thinking, and Feeling) are of particular interest to us at this time because that is where

Exhibit 3.2 Personality Type Distribution of CEOs

ISTJ	ISFJ	INFJ	INTJ	Dichotomous Preferences:		
n = 4	n = 0	n = 0	n = 3	Extrovert n = 36	(71%)	
(7.8%)	(0.0%)	(0.0%)	(5.9%)	Introvert n = 15	(29%)	
+ + + + + +			+ + + + + +	Sensor n = 19	(37%)	
+ +				iNtuitive n = 32	(63%)	
				Thinking n = 38	(75%)	
				Feeling n = 13	(25%)	
ISTP	ISFP	INFP	INTP			
n = 0	n = 3	n = 3	n = 2	Judging n = 34	(67%)	
(0.0%)	(5.9%)	(5.9%)	(3.9%)	Perceiving n = 17	(30%)	
	+ + + + + +	+ + + + + +	+ + + +	Pairs and Temperaments:		
				IJ n = 07	(14%)	
				IP n = 08	(16%)	
				EP n = 09	(18%)	
ESTP	ESFP	ENFP	ENTP	EJ n = 27	(53%)	
n = 1	n = 0	n = 2	n = 6	ST n = 12	(23%)	
(2.0%)	(0.0%)	(3.9%)	(11.8%)	SF n = 05	(10%)	
+ +		+ + + +	+ + + + + +	NF n = 08	(16%)	
			+ + + + + +	NT n = 26	(51%)	
				SJ n = 13	(25%)	
				SP n = 04	(08%)	
				NP n = 13	(25%)	
				NJ n = 21	(41%)	
ESTJ	ESFJ	ENFJ	ENTJ	TJ n = 29	(57%)	
				TP n = 09	(18%)	
n = 7	n = 2	n = 3	n= 15	FP n = 08	(16%)	
(13.7%)	(3.9%)	(5.9%)	(29.4%)	FJ n = 05	(10%)	
+ + + + + +	+ + + +	+ + + + + +	+ + + + + +	IN n = 08	(16%)	
+ + + + + +			+ + + + + +	EN n = 26	(51%)	
+ +			+ + + + + +	IS n = 07	(14%)	
			+ + + + + +	ES n = 10	(20%)	
			+ + + +			

NOTE: N = 51; + = 1% of N.

the shadow may be found. Just as we have preferred personality functions, there are complementary, nonpreferred functions. In other words, iNtuitive, Thinking types' less preferred functions are Sensing and Feeling. Notably, the less preferred functions, according to Jung, provide the clues for accessing your shadow.

Jung and other type theorists believe that the way to work with one's shadow is through the exercise of the third and fourth personality functions, because these reside in the unconscious. Exhibit 3.3 identi-

Exhibit 3.3 MBTI Type Table with Functional Type Development Sequence Along With Exemplar

ISTJ	ISFJ	INFJ	INTJ

Dominant:Sensing
Auxiliary: Thinking
Tertiary: Feeling
Inferior: iNtuition
 	
Example: Robert
         Masters
	Dominant:Sensing
	Auxiliary: Feeling
	Tertiary: Thinking
	Inferior: iNtuition
		Dominant:iNtuition
		Auxiliary: Feeling
		Tertiary: Thinking
		Inferior: Sensing
			Dominant:iNtuition
			Auxiliary: Thinking
			Tertiary: Feeling
			Inferior: Sensing
			
			Example: Richard
			         Farr

ISTP	**ISFP**	**INFP**	**INTP**

Dominant:Thinking
Auxiliary: Sensing
Tertiary: iNtuition
Inferior: Feeling
	Dominant:Feeling
	Auxiliary: Sensing
	Tertiary: iNtuition
	Inferior: Thinking
		Dominant:Feeling
		Auxiliary: iNtuition
		Tertiary: Sensing
		Inferior: Thinking
		
		Example: Randy
		         Maxwell
			Dominant:Thinking
			Auxiliary: iNtuition
			Tertiary: Sensing
			Inferior: Feeling
			
			Example: Joe
			         Henderson

ESTP	**ESFP**	**ENFP**	**ENTP**

Dominant:Sensing
Auxiliary: Thinking
Tertiary: Feeling
Inferior: iNtuition
	Dominant:Sensing
	Auxiliary: Feeling
	Tertiary: Thinking
	Inferior: iNtuition
		Dominant:iNtuition
		Auxiliary: Feeling
		Tertiary: Thinking
		Inferior: Sensing
		
		Example: Michael
		         Breen
			Dominant:iNtuition
			Auxiliary: Thinking
			Tertiary: Feeling
			Inferior: Sensing
			
			Example: Ray
			         Zuckerman

ESTJ	**ESFJ**	**ENFJ**	**ENTJ**
Dominant:Thinking Auxiliary: Sensing Tertiary: iNtuition Inferior: Feeling Example: Steven Zolte	Dominant:Feeling Auxiliary: Sensing Tertiary: iNtuition Inferior: Thinking	Dominant:Feeling Auxiliary: iNtuition Tertiary: Sensing Inferior: Thinking	Dominant:Thinking Auxiliary: iNtuition Tertiary: Sensing Inferior: Feeling

fies the consciously used first and second mental functions (i.e., dominant and auxiliary) as well as the unconsciously used third and fourth mental functions (i.e., tertiary and inferior) for each of the 16 personality types. According to type theory, children, adolescents, and young adults are likely to engage in activities that express the preferred dominant and auxiliary functions. However, older adults after midlife may choose activities to help develop their less preferred tertiary and inferior functions (Corlett & Millner, 1993; Provost, 1990). We will explore this further at the conclusion of the chapter in the shadow-work section.

Case Studies of CEOs' Personalities

Surprisingly, not one of the seven CEOs had the same personality type as the other participants in my field study. As a result, we are able to get a relatively broad perspective on nearly half of the personality types as well as in-depth insights into the personalities of these men in leadership positions (see Exhibit 3.3 for actual dispersion). Listed below is an in-depth discussion of the personality types of each of the seven CEOs who participated in this study, grouped by functional preferences.

SF Types: The Friendly Doers

SF people constitute 31.3% of the American adult population (Hammer & Mitchell, 1996), but only 10% of our sample of CEOs. This group of people prefers the practical, sensible, and concrete way of being, and they are very people oriented. Because they are mainly interested in the facts they can collect with their five senses, they do not have much interest in abstract principles or theories. They tend to be very warm and friendly. In the second half of life, they must begin dealing with their less preferred NT (iNtuitive, Thinking) functions (Myers & McCaulley, 1993).

Unfortunately, none of our field interviews was with a CEO with an SF personality type. Although this was not unexpected, based on our limited sample and the rarity of this type in a CEO's role, it is interesting to speculate why so few people with an SF personality type assume CEO responsibilities. On one hand, this type of person may not aspire to this role in organizations, because it historically put a premium on an ability to theorize and abstract from experience, and these skills do not come easily to an SF person. On the other hand, this is the most common personality type for women (Hammer & Mitchell, 1996); and it could be due to bias in the workplace (i.e., the infamous "glass ceiling"). Regardless of the reason, SF personalities are relatively rare in the CEO's position, and our research confirms this.

ST Types: The Practical Thinkers

ST people constitute 36.8% of the American public (Hammer & Mitchell, 1996) and made up 23% of our CEO sample. They rely primarily on sensing when they collect data and thinking for processing that data. Their main interests focus on facts, because facts can be collected and verified by tasks accomplished through the senses—by seeing, hearing, touching, counting, weighing, and measuring. The ST types typically approach decisions through impersonal analysis; they trust thinking, with its step-by-step logical process of reasoning from cause to effect, from premise to conclusion. In the second half of life, these ST types must begin to deal with their less preferred NF (iNtuitive, Feeling) tendencies (Myers & McCaulley, 1993; Myers & Myers, 1993). There were two CEOs who participated in our field research with the ST preference: Robert Masters and Steven Zolte.

Robert Masters (ISTJ). Robert is an *I*ntroverted, *S*ensing, *T*hinking, and *J*udging type. The ISTJ is a loyal and dutiful person who is strongly committed to ensuring the security and safety of his family and organization (Myers, 1993). Perhaps this loyalty is why Robert stayed with the organization when the firm was in bankruptcy and close to closing its doors. Similarly, it may also explain why he assumed the CEO's position even when the firm's future looked uncertain and the board of directors had demoted him previously.

The ISTJ person likes to be organized, systematic, analytic, and scheduled (Hirsch & Kummerow, 1990). True to type, Robert was ready for our interview at exactly the time that was predetermined. His responses to the interview questions were mostly logical and showed a preoccupation with cause-and-effect thinking. This type of person pays attention to details and makes decisions accordingly. Observe the following excerpt from our interview, as Robert precisely recounted the details surrounding the bankruptcy experience of his firm:

I'm not so sure that we shouldn't have filed for Chapter 11 protection earlier than we did, but you can get into a Chapter 11 situation and not get out very easily. Nationally, I'm told that about 9% of the companies that file for Chapter 11 make it out with the reorganized plan; all the rest of them are converted to Chapter 7. The courts in our state have a reputation of being tougher than average, and I'm told by local attorneys that about 5% actually have their plans approved. In October of '95, we did file for bankruptcy protection and on February 28, we had a plan for reorganization approved.

The ISTJ type often is comfortable with rules and regulations (Myers, 1993). Robert thrived in the environmental services industry, with its extensive and complex rules and regulations. It may also explain why he was so invested in having numerical objectives for himself and the rest of the company in the early part of his career. Starting out as a sales manager, he loved hitting his sales targets, and he was constantly tinkering with the appropriate set of rules to guide the efforts of his subordinates.

As mentioned previously, the ST type must start to deal with his less preferred NF tendencies. At the age of 62, Robert had some opportunities to work with his shadow. Based on our interview, there was some evidence to suggest that he had done some work. In this case, shadow work involved becoming more sensitive and caring for his employees later on in his career through engagement with his less preferred feeling function coupled with some intuition. Here is his story:

> There was a period early in my career when I looked almost exclusively at my subordinates' performance. I evaluated them on what they produced, and it didn't matter to me why or why not you didn't produce. You know, if your wife is sick or your kid is failing or something, I didn't see it as my problem; that was your problem. In recent years, I am more sensitive to that, and what I find is people will sense that and start to come to you. It is amazing; I don't understand how it happens but it does. For example, now people will drop by at lunchtime and say, "I want to talk to you about something." I had a lady come to talk to me about a problem the other day. Her granddaughter had abandoned her two small kids—her great-grandchildren. She came to me looking for advice on whether she should try to get custody of the children. In the past, this never would have happened; and if it did, I would have discouraged such discussions. Now I do it because I care so deeply for my workers. It feels good, but I don't understand the experience at all.

Robert did not speak of the difficulty of making such a transition, but he did notice the energy release by opening himself to less preferred parts of himself. This is the result of shadow work with one's inferior function, in this case, his intuition, which is open to nonlinear thinking and uncertain cause and effect. Furthermore, he opened himself to his tertiary function, his feeling function, as he sought harmony with "his people" and valued them for who they were, not what they could produce.

Steven Zolte (ESTJ). Steven is an *E*xtroverted, *S*ensing, *T*hinking, and *J*udging type. The ESTJ types usually direct thinking skills to the outer world rather than to the inner world of personal ideas and ideals. They are often the most tough-minded of all types as they are intellectually active but emotionally passive. At work, this gives them a decided advantage in productivity and efficiency (Pedersen, 1993). True to type, Steven earned two graduate degrees while simultaneously rising in the ranks of a *Fortune* 500 firm in the early part of his career. He was given profit-center responsibility early on and was able to "improve the numbers each and every time." The following discussion, as Steven described his work habits, was most telling:

> When I went to work at (company name), people would wander in between 8:00 and 8:30, and they would wander out between 4:30 and 5:00. I got there at 8:00 a.m. sharp and got the job done. While other people would stand around drinking coffee during the day, I was working. So my output was two to three times what theirs was.

ESTJs are extremely goal- and task-oriented. They direct high levels of energy to planning, action, and the implementation of goals (Hirsch & Kummerow, 1990). Consistent with this, Steven set a goal of becoming a CEO of a billion-dollar publicly held firm while he was earning his MBA degree at the age of 28. At age 50, he was well on the way to fulfilling his goal—he was the CEO of a publicly held firm with over $700 million in revenues and growing 15% per year.

In dealing with others, ESTJs tend to be straightforward. They have a no-nonsense approach and often seem emotionally cool if not distant (Myers, 1993). Illustrating this trait, Steven recounted the following: "If you engage in overt sexual harassment in my firm, you are gone. I've had six managers, each with more than 20 years of experience, who didn't understand that—they no longer work here."

In the second half of life, STs have an opportunity to embrace their less-preferred side, their NF tendencies. For Steven at age 50, this appears to be explored through his having had a mentor. Observe how he describes this feeling-oriented mentor:

The first guy that I worked for in the business world was a great guy. In fact, he was my mentor for about 4 years. He really is a great guy, a very caring, feeling individual. He taught me that one doesn't have to be a hard ass all the time; there is a time to show employees that you are caring about them and interested in some things more than just the business. That stuff doesn't come easily for me, but he showed me that it can work and can be effective.

Unfortunately, there was no other indication in our lengthy interview that Steven was wrestling with his shadow; nor was there any indication that he had begun to draw from his NF energies. Of course, only Steven knows where that activity is going, but his disclosure of his mentor's role-modeling could be indicative of some shadow work.

NF Type: The Imaginative Developers

The NF type is the least common type in the American public, with 15.8% of people showing this disposition (Hammer & Mitchell, 1996). In our survey of CEOs, 16% tested as this type—almost identical to the proportion of the general public. NF people look at the world and see possibilities (intuition), especially as it relates to people and relationships. Given to idealistic concerns, they often see opportunities and work to make the world a better place (Myers & McCaulley, 1993). There were two CEOs with the NF preference: Michael Breen and Randy Maxwell.

Michael Breen (ENFP). Michael is an *E*xtroverted, i*N*tuitive, *F*eeling, and *P*erceiving type. For ENFPs, life is a creative adventure full of exciting possibilities (Hirsch & Kummerow, 1990). For example, Michael, commenting on his own adventure, states, "Ten years ago, I was a banker. Five years ago, I was a business executive. Today, I am a leader of a business with tremendous potential."

ENFPs rely on their intuition, as it is their dominant function. Furthermore, people of this type are often innovative and enjoy initiating projects and directing great energy into getting them under way (Myers, 1993). Illustrating this characteristic, Michael states,

I do most things by my intuition. I often get an idea by imagining a new way; and then I float it by my team, often concluding,

"We need to go here." Then, they inevitably say, "Well, where is the evidence to go there?" And I say, "Gee, I don't have any evidence for you why we should go there, but I still think that's where we ought to go. So let's start down that path and test it out." We usually do test out my ideas after that. Fortunately, my intuition is often proven right when the evidence starts coming in. I have learned to trust my intuition, and it has served me well.

These types of people are keenly perceptive of people and the world around them (Myers, 1993). True to type, Michael comments, "Finance and the numbers matter greatly in this business; but that is not what motivates people—it is matters of the heart and emotion that drive people to excellence, in my opinion."

ENFPs readily find meaning in small events and see connections that others often don't see (Hirsch & Kummerow, 1990). Commenting on his firm's progress, Michael says,

Well, in a publicly held corporation, obviously the financial results are important; and those are encouraging, and they're heading in the right direction. A lot of positive things are happening on that front. But those can be sort of short-term in nature also. And so I really need to look at what's happening long term in this corporation that is going to sustain that kind of profitability and growth. And what you really have to be able to look at is attitudes. Attitudes are subtle; but if you look for them and think about them, you can learn a lot.

ENFPs value harmony and goodwill (Myers, 1993). For example, Michael continually emphasized teamwork and his role within his top management team. Notably, he often gave credit to his team for the strong results of this firm:

Our bank has had some strong financial results recently, and I am getting all the credit on Wall Street. But I've got to tell you, I am very much a "right person in the right places" kind of guy. That was the first thing that I did when I came here by putting the right people in the right places. Then I let them do what they do best and just made sure that the vision is on track and the teamwork is there. I've got the easiest job here. I really do [laughing].

It is natural for ENFPs to give less attention to their nonpreferred sensing and thinking parts (Corlett & Millner, 1993). As a result, details and practical action are not their strong suit. When asked what the firm's specific financial goals are, Michael replied, "I honestly don't know; that is what my CFO is paid to pay attention to."

At the conclusion of the interview, Michael indicated that his biggest struggle was that he was not putting in enough time with his young children. Working 60 hours a week, he worried whether he invested the time and energy in their lives as he should. In love with his work and supremely confident in his role as CEO, he struggled with the balance between his personal and professional life. At the relatively young age of 43, perhaps this struggle is, or will be, the doorway to his shadow work. However, embracing his less preferred ST functions may transform his relationship with his children so that this struggle disappears. Only time, mixed with shadow work, will tell.

Randy Maxwell (INFP). Randy is an *I*ntroverted, i*N*tuitive, *F*eeling, and *P*erceiving type. INFPs usually have a set of deeply felt principles that guide their interactions and decisions (Myers, 1993). One of Randy's primary guiding principles is that of determination and perseverance. Consequently, one of his personal mottos is: "Success is moving from failure to failure without losing your motivation."

Moral commitment is usually very important to INFPs (Myers, 1993). Randy repeatedly spoke of the importance of being a good "steward" of resources and "serving" his employees and customers well and in a principled manner. He also cared deeply about business ethics and had the battle scars to show for it. He recounted one particular incident:

We had to remove, for ethical lapses, the founder of our company—first out of the position of chairmanship and then, ultimately, off the board. Because we set high standards and I have a good board of directors that also operates by those same standards, we were able to act. It was not easy nor was it a pleasant thing to do; but it was one where there was good commonality among the board, and we didn't need to sit around and debate what is right or wrong. Now the attempt was made to be fair to the individual, and we were. But lines were crossed that shouldn't have, and we had to act.

In addition, INFPs are fascinated by opportunities to explore the complexities of life (Hirsch & Kummerow, 1990). For example, Randy designed a rather elaborate goal-setting process and performance-review system in his firm. He described it as follows:

It is sort of an MBO (management-by-objectives) concept. And we use the ratings of "basic" and "target" and "outstanding." Basic is designed to be nonthreatening at the 75% to 80% level. If you achieve a basic level of performance, you have assured yourself one more year of work. The target level of performance is a bit more of a stretch, typically at 100% effort and results. Outstanding is the great leap forward, something like 150% effort and results. Of course, hitting these levels brings higher levels of compensation, which we tailor to individual needs and interests. It is an iterative process that involves the employee and his or her boss and often others involved with hitting one's targets. And then the numbers start to fall into place, and we've built the numbers back up. For example, I want to go from $22 million to $30 million in sales next year. From that goal, other goals are derived. Furthermore, we make all goals public so folks can see how they stack up against others in their negotiations. They can go to HR at any time and look up anyone's set of goals. It is a system that is highly interrelated and constantly being refined. . . . The important thing is to get buy-in and create opportunity and that is what this system does. . . . I think a lot about creating an environment where people can do their best.

Despite this elaborate performance-review system, INFPs often find structures and rules confining (Myers, 1993). True to type, Randy declared, "The absence of a policy is the best policy we can get away with." He is constantly trying to boil expectations down to their simplest essence, while eliminating unnecessary bureaucracy and formalities. He states,

There is only one thing that matters in this company, which is achieving goals to the maximum level at the highest standards.

I constantly push that idea. And then I have some fun, just to get the point across. I also say what we don't care about. We don't care about politics; we don't care about organizational charts; we don't care about marital status; and we certainly don't care if you are gay, heterosexual, or whatever. And so people are really open about this, as a result, because they know it doesn't matter.

This type of person often values relationships based on depth, authenticity, true connection, and mutual growth (Myers, 1993). Randy states,

It doesn't matter to me what kind of clothes you wear, what kind of car you drive, or even when you come and go from work. I want to be able to laugh with my employees and create some meaningful work relationships where we are all able to perform to the best of our abilities. I love my work here and the people that work here.

Being an INFP, Randy's shadow tendencies are in the sensing and thinking area. He disclosed that he had to face all his fears and demons in his early 20s, while serving as a helicopter pilot in the height of the Vietnam War. Interestingly, he is convinced that by developing his "attention to details" (i.e., sensing) and "planning ahead" (i.e., thinking), his chances of returning safely and completing the mission were greatly enhanced. Using these new skills as well as "keeping a positive attitude" (i.e., intuition) and "taking good care of his flight crew" (i.e., feeling), he was able to dramatically improve his chances of returning home "with both arms, legs, and head intact." Thus, at the relatively young age of 47, Randy appeared to have engaged his shadow as a result of "looking death in the eye and making some changes in my life."

NT Types: The Logical Theorists

Among American adults, this type constitutes 16.1% of the population (Hammer & Mitchell, 1996). Notably, 51% of our sample were revealed to be this type. Clearly, the NT executive is the most common type for CEOs, and previous research supports this finding. For example, Ginn and Sexton (1989) found that the CEOs of rapid growth Inc. 500 firms are predominantly NT types (51%). Similarly, Roach (1982) found the same proclivity for the NT type in the executive ranks in larger organizations.

What could explain this overrepresentation of the NT personality type at the top of the organization? Reynierse (1993) speculated that abstraction and relatively long time horizons allow NTs to shine in the CEO's role. Walck (1992) theorized that those with a broader view (i.e., intuition) who can deal with things objectively (i.e., thinking) are more likely to aspire to a top-level executive position. Whatever the reason, the CEO's position is most commonly occupied by the NT type. There were three CEOs in our field study with the NT preference: Joseph Henderson, Richard Farr, and Raymond Zuckerman.

Joseph Henderson (INTP). Joseph is an *I*ntroverted, i*N*tuitive, *T*hinking, and *P*erceiving personality type. INTPs are often independent problem solvers who excel at providing a detached, concise analysis of an idea or situation. They usually ask hard questions, challenging others and themselves to find new, logical approaches (Myers, 1993). Joseph demonstrated this behavior often—by concluding that major change was coming in his industry and sounding the alarm to his fellow executives, by redirecting his energies when things weren't working out, and by analyzing the causes of change, not just seeing the symptoms of change.

INTPs are often engaged in a continual search for underlying principles and logical structures (Hirsch & Kummerow, 1990). Joseph explained,

> In my search for controlling costs without sacrificing the quality of health care, I kept looking for the missing piece to the puzzle and a framework for attacking that puzzle. To me, the missing piece is the physician and the framework is a trusting relationship between the business of health care and the physician. We are still refining that framework, but I think we are onto something big.

This type often highly values intelligence and competence (Hirsch & Kummerow, 1990). Reflecting on initial start-up attempts, Joseph explained,

> Since I wanted to try out an unproven concept, I thought that I had to get some big names in health care to join me. So I

approached the big consultants and prominent executives in the industry who had the experience and smarts to make this thing work. But it wasn't working out and the big names seemed invested in their own endeavors. And so I stopped recruiting executives for a while and did some thinking about where this was all going. A few days later, I was reading a book by Chuck Swindoll, *A Quest for Character,* and I was sitting there thinking. In that book, he says: "I don't even know why I am writing this, but maybe there is somebody out there trying to start a business. If you are, don't go for the big names. Go for people that you know are comers in the field with absolute competence, people with unquestioned integrity, and have the capacity to love one another." I followed his advice and things really started moving then.

INTPs often see inconsistencies and lack of logic very quickly (Myers, 1993). True to type, Joe states,

All my career, I have been concerned about the cost of health care. Increasingly, others are concerned, too. However, much of the explanations for the high and growing cost of health care in this country is shallow and just touches the surface. Furthermore, many of the solutions to the health care crisis are contradictory and just don't make sense.

This type of person is often tolerant of a wide range of behavior until their ruling principles are challenged (Myers, 1993). Commenting on his decision-making style, Joe explained,

It's very rare that I will make a decision independent of my team. Most of the time, we will reach a consensus. And many times, I will submit to the group's wishes. But occasionally, when an issue involves something that I believe strongly about, I will say something like: "Guys, I hear you, but we are not going to do that." And they respect that, because I don't do it very often; and they know that I won't budge when I believe strongly in something. Most important, we make good decisions jointly and the relationships are solid.

In his mid-40s, Joe was executive of a multimillion-dollar business and happily married and in good health. It all seemed rosy, and then "the bottom fell out"—he was fired from his job, and his wife of 25 years asked for a divorce. In Joe's own words,

> I was too comfortable, and so I ended up on the seat of my pants. I found myself in my mid-40s, you know, in effect losing my family, losing my job—from a time of thinking I had it all. So what it did was to put me in a position to say clearly to myself, "I am not in control. I am not pretending to be in control. Please, God, put me where You want me, and I will do my best." And once I reached that point, then He just began to create—a new person and a new business around that new person. It is amazing what happens when you give up control to God.

For Joseph, engaging his shadow was a time of giving up control to God. At the age of 54, he appeared to be open to more and more potential skills and competencies, paradoxically, by letting go. We will discuss this phenomenon further in subsequent chapters.

Richard Farr (INTJ). Richard is an *I*ntroverted, i*N*tuitive, *T*hinking, and *J*udging type. INTJs are highly independent personalities with strong visions of what the organization can be. They are often willing to reorganize the entire system when they feel it isn't working properly (Myers, 1993). For example, Richard helped to found this bank around a new and innovative set of ideals of what a community bank could be.

INTJs often have a difficult time letting go of impractical ideas (Myers, 1993). True to type, Richard had some clear ideas how a young man should behave, but his 21- and 18-year-old sons would have none of those ideas. Like many parents, Richard struggled with them "going down fool's hill"; but unlike many parents of teenagers, he still thought he could control their behavior.

People with INTJ personalities often work hard to achieve their goals (Hirsch & Kummerow, 1990). In Richard's own words,

> I am a workaholic. I work long and hard; I really don't do much other than spend time with my family and my work. There are some things I need to accomplish before I die, and I am bent on achieving those things.

INTJs are conceptual people who like to draw insights from one experience and relate it to other experiences (Hirsch & Kummerow, 1990). For example, Richard asserted that work and family are interspersed for him:

A lot of times when I am dealing with people problems at work I can often look back and take things that I learned from raising my children to see what to do. Also, sometimes I learn things that work on the job that I take back to my family. Each activity feeds each other.

INTJs often think long term (Hirsch & Kummerow, 1990). Discussing the top management team of which he was a member, Richard described himself as follows: "I am more of a dreamer—I'd like to think that I am a visionary, but that is for others to determine. Of the three of us, I am the longest thinker. Together, we make a pretty good team."

INTJs are very comfortable with cause-effect thinking and theorizing (Myers, 1993). When asked why his bank had been so successful thus far, Richard replied,

I think that there are several reasons for success, but one of the key variables is the people that we hire. You know, banking is a people business; and we really don't go out and hire a lot of people that we don't know. We hire people that, first of all, can make it happen and, second of all, have integrity and honor.

INTJs are often private and reserved and hard to get to know (Myers & Myers, 1993). Richard noted,

Our chairman is a very outgoing guy. Every day, he goes through the bank and shakes hands with the employees and yucks it up with them. He is really good at that. In contrast, that doesn't come easily for me. I can see what a difference it makes, mixing with the troops, but it is hard and a bit of a stretch for me to do the same thing.

Finally, INTJs handle challenges to their ideas very well because this is their realm and they are confident in that area (Hirsch & Kummerow, 1990). Comparing his style to other CEOs, Richard stated,

I have seen lots of CEOs surround themselves with "yes men," but that never led to something good. Often, it comes back to haunt the CEO—he doesn't have enough diversity of ideas. I think you have to surround yourself with people who challenge you. That is sometimes hard to do. Even in dealing with subordinates, it is especially uncomfortable when they disagree with you. But you have to do it to survive and do well.

It was not clear from our interview where Richard, at the age of 48, was in dealing with his less preferred personality functions. It is possible that most of his inner work is coming from battles with his younger sons, but there was too little data to support that speculation. As indicated previously, it takes a while to get to know this type, and disclosure of inner struggles does not come quickly for this type of person.

Raymond Zuckerman (ENTP). Raymond is an Extroverted, iNtuitive, Thinking, and Perceiving type. Like most NTs, this type likes complex challenges and enjoys taking initiative to spur things on. Furthermore, the ENTP type is not very bureaucratic and likes to encourage autonomy (Hirsch & Kummerow, 1990). Illustrating this characteristic, Raymond declared,

My father said you should treat every customer that comes through your door as if they were coming into your home. That is basically our motto and philosophy around here. . . . That is oversimplifying it somewhat. Obviously, I could give you a lot of corporate rhetoric, but that is what it all boils down to. I have found that you have to keep things simple and focused to get folks to take initiative.

ENTPs are spontaneous and fairly adaptable types (Myers, 1993). In our interview, Raymond cracked jokes, ate ice cream, received phone calls, and teased employees walking by his office, and his ideas zigged and zagged. He spoke about the need for change in his company and how that was a struggle in a firm of 24,000 employees. Overall, Raymond was the most playful CEO that we interviewed.

Despite this spontaneity, ENTPs can be brash and blunt, sometimes even abusive (Myers, 1993). Raymond recounted,

When I walk into a store that is dirty, I tell the manager in front of his subordinates: "Please don't ever invite me to your house for dinner." And he often replies, "Why is that?" And I say: "Because if you work in such a filthy place as this, I don't want to see what you live in." Shortly thereafter, I often have to fire that manager.

Raymond disclosed that it was "lonely at the top," and this may have been the doorway into his shadow. He stated,

Everybody aspires to get to the top. But once they get there, a lot of them can't handle it. First of all, you often get out of the things you most like to do. Next, the buck stops here, and that can really weigh you down. Finally, all your relationships change with the board and your top management team. There is more formality, and the business often must come first. It is a terrible job, but someone has to do it [laughing].

To cope with his loneliness, Raymond started signing birthday cards to all his employees, or associates as he calls them, when he became CEO. At first, he just started doing it to see where it would go. In his own words, "it worked fine when the firm had a mere 6,000 employees." However, the employment at his firm grew to 24,000, and Raymond found his signature limit was 10,000. So he purchased a machine that signs 14,000 signatures, and he signs the remaining 10,000 every year. In the process, he has gotten to know more and more of his associates, and a new and special relationship has emerged, "particularly with the hourly people." Thus, at the age of 62, Raymond has begun dealing with his sensing and feeling functions through the relatively novel approach of personally signing birthday cards for his employees.

Summing Up

One important aspect of executive character is one's personality. In this chapter, I used Jungian concepts of personality and the MBTI instrument to show the varying gifts of the various 16 personality types (Myers & Myers, 1993). In so doing, we discover that there are a wide variety of personality types serving in the CEO's role, but the majority of the CEOs operate with intuitive and thinking personality preferences.

This personality theory also offers insights into the less preferred "shadow" aspects of personality. According to Jung, it is these less preferred, shadowy aspects of ourselves that must be integrated into our lives in the second half of life. This is often difficult to do, but the rewards are many. The clearest examples of shadow work came from CEOs in their 60s who had "let go" of the illusion that they were in control. Paradoxically, this act of letting go gave them more energy and power and responsibility in their lives.

Individual Shadow Work With Personality

Jung believed that the first half of life should be focused on discovering and honoring your inborn personality preferences, whereas the second half of life should be focused on exploring and honoring one's nonpreferred, or shadow, tendencies. Although it varies from person to person, most people, Jung found, shifted "from the morning to the afternoon" of their lives, often between the ages of 35 and 40.

1. Begin by getting information on your personality preferences, using the MBTI, administered by a competent and certified MBTI trainer. If you are under the age of 30, your task is to honor the "gifts" of your unique personality in the world around you. If you are over the age of 30 and you are clear about your own personality, now may be the time to consciously start your shadow work.

2. Once you know your preferred personality type, you know by default what your nonpreferred type is. According to Jung, this is where the shadow exists, and, hence, it is where the "gold" is. Refer to Exhibit 3.3 to learn what your dominant, auxiliary, tertiary, and inferior types are. Your shadow is accessed by engaging the tertiary and inferior types. You engage the unconscious through being with it, not consciously doing something to it. This is best achieved through the following means:

Exhibit 3.4 Potential Play Activities Suggested by Provost (1990)

ISTJ	ISFJ	INFJ	INTJ
Take a psychology course just for fun	Take a course in watercolor technique, experimenting with abstracts and landscapes	Practice a complicated piano piece that requires repetition of difficult passages	Take up a fast-paced, physically intense sport of handball
ISTP	**ISFP**	**INFP**	**INTP**
Attend small group discussions on abstract subjects where each person shares personal reactions to the ideas	Tinker with a home computer with financial planning software	Make friends with Thinking types and engage them in analytical debates	Prepare dinners for friends and share experiences and confidences during the meal
ESTP	**ESFP**	**ENFP**	**ENTP**
Join a local theater group and perform several Shakespearean productions	Dabble in parapsychology, reading and attending programs on astrology and numerology	Become interested in nature photography in which one takes closeups of flower petals and drops of dew	Learn to dance exuberantly
ESTJ	**ESFJ**	**ENFJ**	**ENTJ**
Attend art shows with friends and discuss one's reactions to the artwork	Read science fiction, then discuss it with a teenager	Participate in the technical aspects of building a house or repairing a car	Go fishing with a friend and take pleasure even if no fish are caught

a. Find some leisure activity that requires you to use your less preferred mental functions.

b. Find a creative outlet that requires you to use your less preferred mental functions.

c. Take more pauses in your work day; meditate regularly; daydream more.

3. Judith Provost (1990) has an excellent book on playing with your shadow. Exhibit 3.4 has some examples of playing with less preferred functions. Review this list and brainstorm additional play activities for your particular type.

Personal Values of Executive Leaders

Confusion and lack of clear values on the part of the young puts an even greater burden on their elders to reflect on their own values. If adults in a society do not have some considered notion of their values, there would seem to be little hope for young people. It is especially important that individuals have clearly articulated values in a time of rapid change.
— Cavanaugh, 1976, p. 186

A wide variety of researchers have asserted that leadership is a value-laden activity. For example, Edgar Schein (1990) argued that the essence of leadership is the ability to oversee and manage the organization's values, particularly when the current values are dysfunctional. Similarly, Peter Vaill (1991) argued that "leadership is the articulation of new values and the energetic presentation of them to those whose actions are affected by them" (p. 55). And in studies of executive development, research has shown that one of the most important things to learn is one's own values and the values of the organization (McCall, Lombardo, & Morrison, 1988).

Values are deep-seated, pervasive standards that influence almost every aspect of a person's life (Schmidt & Posner, 1986) and guide action within organizations (Guth & Taguiri, 1965). Knowing one's values is important because values establish standards of behavior (Rokeach, 1973) and are remarkably stable over time (Rokeach & Ball-Rokeach, 1989). In the case of executive leaders, having clear personal values is an essential precursor to identifying and supporting the values held most dear to the overall organization. Furthermore, clarity about personal values should make it easier to identify similarities and differences in values throughout the rest of the organization. Notably, value congruence, or "shared values," within an organization has been shown to be an essential component of organizational effectiveness (Collins & Porras, 1994; Peters & Waterman, 1982). However, the larger and more heterogeneous the organization, the more difficult it is to achieve value congruence (Vaill, 1991).

Clearly, organizational values and effective executive leadership are linked closely to each other (Selznick, 1957). Cavanaugh (1976) notes,

> Empirical studies of business people have found them to be ambitious, achievement-oriented, disciplined, and adaptable. These values were inculcated largely by mothers, who were the more influential parent. . . . Executives' goals and values are often determined for them. After mid-career, however, executives sometimes begin to probe their own personal values. (p. 101)

The purpose of this chapter is to explore the values of current executives in leadership positions and compare those value systems to the general public. Next, this book offers ideas for clarifying and adjusting your values to prepare yourself for aligning your values to the overall organization's values, recognizing that high-performing organizations must reconcile conflicting organizational values (Quinn, 1991).

The Nature of Personal Values

Having stated the importance of clarifying personal values, it is useful to distinguish between *public* and *private* values. Sometimes, individuals identify certain values as being near and dear to their hearts (i.e., private values); however, their actual behavior (i.e., public values) indicates otherwise. What could account for this discrepancy between a person's public and private values? One possibility is the person knows his preferred values but realizes that these values conflict with the organization's primary values and suppresses his opinions and behaviors for fear of reprisals (Bartolome, 1989). As a result, the public values are merely rationalizations or aspirations (Schein, 1990). Another possibility is that the person has weak or transient values and does not know his core values. These people would rather adopt external, and often foreign, values rather than investigating their own core beliefs (Covey, 1989). In either case, the individual has generated an internal conflict that must eventually be reconciled.

A second notion that is important to recognize about personal values is that we can often hold several different values simultaneously. Because values sometimes conflict within us, we must often set priorities among them. Thus, values operate as a "system" within us that some believe is ordered within a personal hierarchy. Furthermore, value systems can change over time as a direct result of social influences, personal maturation, or both (Rokeach, 1973).

While it is possible for value systems to change over time, they sometimes remain the same over a lifetime, and if they do change, they do so very slowly. There are two possible explanations for this. First, values often remain in the unconscious mind, determining a person's behavior, but because they are not consciously chosen, these values are not readily apparent to their holder (Rokeach, 1973). Second, although some people do consciously identify their most important values, over time, they begin to focus on other matters of life. "As values begin to be taken for granted, they gradually become beliefs and assumptions and drop out of consciousness" (Schein, 1990, p. 16). In sum, personal values can change over time, but if they do, it is usually a gradual process.

A third notion that is helpful when thinking about personal values is that there are two basic types of values, which have been called *instrumental* and *terminal* values (Rokeach, 1973). Instrumental values refer to our preferred modes of behavior. In contrast, terminal values are the end states that we seek in life. Milton Rokeach identified 18 terminal and 18 instrumental values that exist across generations and nationalities and genders and occupations. The Rokeach Value Survey (RVS) has been used extensively to explore employee motivation

(Brown, 1976), ethical choices (McCabe, Dukerich, & Dutton, 1991), cross-cultural differences (Kamakura & Mazzon, 1991), differences between entrepreneurs and managers (Fagenson, 1993), and even customer segments (Kahle & Kennedy, 1988). Because of the extensive use of the RVS, it is a useful approach for examining the values of CEOs.

CEOs' Value Systems

Terminal Values

Exhibit 4.1 lists the aggregate preferences among the terminal values held by the CEO respondents in the general survey. The aggregate preferences were determined by computing a composite index. This index was determined by multiplying each first choice by 5, second choice by 4, third choice by 3, fourth choice by 2, and fifth choice by 1; then, the products were summed into an overall index. With this approach, we learn the relative weight placed on each of the 18 values across all respondents.

Clearly, "a sense of accomplishment" was the most popular value selected by the CEOs, as 84% of them selected this terminal value in their top five, yielding a composite index of 255. The second most popular terminal value was "family security"; 65% selected this value, which earned it a composite index of 206. "Self-respect" was the third most popular terminal value with a composite index of 147, and "salvation" was the fourth most popular terminal value with a composite index of 131.

It is also interesting and informative to examine the least popular terminal values. Notably, "pleasure" was the least popular value, with only two CEOs selecting it, which earned it a composite rating of 5. Also, "a world of beauty" was seldom selected by the CEOs, as it earned a composite index of only 7. Third and fourth from the bottom were "equality" and "social recognition," with each earning a composite index of 8.

Previous research has shown that the values of equality and a world of beauty are in the idealistic terminal values, whereas the values of social recognition and pleasure are in the hedonistic group of terminal values (Crosby, Bitner, & Gill, 1990). In contrast, the values of sense of accomplishment, salvation, and self-respect are in the self-actualization

Exhibit 4.1   CEOs' Aggregate Terminal Values

Value	Not Selected	Top Five	Composite Index[a]	Rank
Sense of accomplishment	15 (16%)	76 (84%)	255	1
Family security	32 (35%)	59 (65%)	206	2
Self-respect	43 (47%)	48 (53%)	147	3
Salvation	58 (64%)	33 (36%)	131	4
Happiness	55 (60%)	36 (40%)	98	5
Wisdom	56 (62%)	35 (38%)	97	6
Freedom	60 (66%)	31 (34%)	86	7
An exciting life	66 (73%)	25 (27%)	74	8
A comfortable life	68 (75%)	23 (25%)	57	9
Mature love	75 (82%)	16 (18%)	47	10
True friendship	72 (79%)	19 (21%)	46	11
Inner harmony	75 (82%)	16 (18%)	37	12
A world at peace	83 (91%)	8 (9%)	19	13
National security	86 (95%)	5 (5%)	11	14
Social recognition	88 (97%)	3 (3%)	8	15
Equality	86 (95%)	5 (5%)	8	15
A world of beauty	87 (96%)	4 (4%)	7	17
Pleasure	89 (98%)	2 (2%)	5	18

$N = 91$.
a. Index computed by multiplying the number of times ranked No. 1 by five; summed with the number of times ranked No. 2 by four; summed with the number of times ranked No. 3 by three; summed with the number of times ranked No. 4 by two; summed with the number of times ranked No. 5 by one.

group while the value of family security lies in the security group of terminal values (Crosby et al., 1990). Thus, we can conclude that the espoused terminal values of CEOs tend to emphasize self-actualization and security more than hedonism and idealism.

Three decades ago, Rokeach (1973) performed a national survey of American adults on their value rankings. Despite the considerable gap in time in data collection periods, it is interesting to compare the general public's values to those of our CEO sample. Exhibit 4.2 compares the CEO terminal value rankings to the general public's terminal value rankings.

Exhibit 4.2 Comparison of CEOs' Terminal Values With American
Adults' Terminal Values

Terminal Value	CEOs' Composite Rank (N = 91)	Adult Americans' Rank[a] (N = 1,409)
Sense of accomplishment	1	10
Family security	2	12
Self-respect	3	5
Salvation	4	8
Happiness	5	4
Wisdom	6	6
Freedom	7	3
An exciting life	8	18
A comfortable life	9	9
Mature love	10	14
True friendship	11	11
Inner harmony	12	13
A world at peace	13	1
National security	14	2
Social recognition	15	16
Equality	16	7
A world of beauty	17	15
Pleasure	18	17

a. Based on a national sample of American adults during the mid-1960s (Rokeach, 1973).

Interestingly, the top four terminal values of the CEOs (i.e., sense
of accomplishment, family security, self-respect, and salvation) are
entirely different from the top four values of the general public (i.e., a
world at peace, national security, freedom, and happiness). One possible explanation for this is that America in the 1970s was engaged in
the Vietnam War and the Cold War with communism; issues of peace,
national security, and freedom were being discussed extensively in the
news media and, hence, influenced the public's values.

A second possible explanation for the differences in values between
CEOs today and the American public of the 1960s is that people are
now less trusting of institutions in the aftermath of the 1960s (Roof,
1993). This was a time of disillusionment when many people felt they
were betrayed by their institutions due to the fighting of wars that they

did not believe in, unjust social systems, and corruption in high places. Consequently, the CEOs of the 1990s are drawn to values that are more focused on their individual lives, whereas the adults of the 1960s were more drawn to values that were focused on their collective well-being.

A third possible explanation for the striking differences is that CEOs are fundamentally different in their value systems from the general adult public. CEOs are elite members of society, and it is not uncommon for the elites to carry different values than the general public. It may be that CEOs are fundamentally different in outlook when compared to the general public.

Instrumental Values

In contrast to terminal values, instrumental values are focused on personal preferences that guide how we live our daily life, not what we are living for. Rokeach (1973) also identified 18 instrumental values; in addition to the terminal values questions, we asked our CEOs to rank their top five instrumental values. The composite rankings across all the CEOs are listed in Exhibit 4.3.

As can be seen from Exhibit 4.3, the preeminent value most often selected by the CEOs sampled is *honest.* About 88% of the CEOs identified honesty as one of their top five instrumental values, yielding a composite index of 340. The second most popular instrumental value identified was *responsible,* but it had a composite index of only 238. Rounding out the top four were *ambitious* and *capable.* Clearly, these publicly espoused instrumental values speak volumes about the CEOs' self-concept and the characteristics sought in others.

It is also interesting to note which values were deemed less important to the CEOs. The least important values were: *obedient, clean, polite,* and *cheerful.* In previous research, all these values are known as the ones dealing with conformity (Crosby et al., 1990). It is evident that conforming values and behaviors are not those most highly valued by CEOs, despite the fact that most employees see this otherwise (Bartolome, 1989).

When comparing the CEOs' values to the values of the general public, we can see that there is remarkable consistency between the two groups' instrumental values (see Exhibit 4.4). Indeed, the top three values of the CEOs are identical to the top three values of the general population (i.e., honest, responsible, and ambitious), despite the 30-

Exhibit 4.3 CEOs' Aggregate Instrumental Values

Instrumental Value	Not Selected	Top Five	Composite Index[a]	Rank
Honest	11 (12%)	80 (88%)	340	1
Responsible	22 (24%)	69 (76%)	238	2
Ambitious	48 (53%)	43 (47%)	120	3
Capable	55 (60%)	36 (40%)	103	4
Imaginative	54 (59%)	37 (41%)	95	5
Courageous	63 (69%)	28 (31%)	72	6
Broadminded	64 (70%)	27 (30%)	66	7
Logical	66 (73%)	25 (27%)	55	8
Independent	73 (80%)	18 (20%)	54	9
Loving	75 (82%)	16 (18%)	41	10
Self-controlled	74 (81%)	17 (19%)	41	10
Helpful	74 (81%)	17 (19%)	36	12
Intellectual	80 (88%)	11 (12%)	30	13
Forgiving	82 (90%)	9 (10%)	26	14
Cheerful	82 (90%)	9 (10%)	18	15
Polite	87 (96%)	4 (4%)	9	16
Clean	88 (97%)	3 (3%)	7	17
Obedient	90 (99%)	1 (1%)	3	18

NOTE: $N = 91$.

a. Index computed by multiplying the number of times ranked No. 1 by five; summed with the number of times ranked No. 2 by four; summed with the number of times ranked No. 3 by three; summed with the number of times ranked No. 4 by two; summed with the number of times ranked No. 5 by one.

year time lag between these two studies. Similarly, the least desired values are quite similar between the two groups. In sum, there appears to be quite a bit of similarity between the instrumental values of CEOs and those of the general public.

We can also compare our CEOs' instrumental values to the instrumental values of other executives at different levels within the organization. Exhibit 4.5 lists our survey results and compares them to data published by Warren Schmidt and Barry Posner (1982). As can be seen from that table, the ranking is remarkably similar when one compares the CEOs' values to the values of the other three levels of executives.

Exhibit 4.4　Comparison of CEOs' Instrumental Values With Adult Americans' Instrumental Values

Instrumental Value	CEOs' Composite Rank (N = 91)	Adult Americans' Rank[a] (N = 1,409)
Honest	1	1
Responsible	2	3
Ambitious	3	2
Capable	4	9
Imaginative	5	18
Courageous	6	6
Broadminded	7	5
Logical	8	17
Independent	9	13
Loving	10	11
Self-controlled	10	10
Helpful	12	7
Intellectual	13	15
Forgiving	14	4
Cheerful	15	12
Polite	16	14
Clean	17	8
Obedient	18	16

a. Based on a national survey of American adults in the mid-1960s (Rokeach, 1973).

Interestingly, the only value that is ranked significantly different by the CEOs is *courageous,* which is ranked far higher by the CEOs than lower level executives. This difference suggests that the CEO must exercise more bravery in executing his duties as compared to other positions within the organization.

Case Studies of CEOs' Personal Values

Robert Masters

The primary terminal values in Robert's life were (in descending order): salvation, freedom, wisdom, self-respect, and a sense of accom-

Exhibit 4.5 Comparison of CEOs' Instrumental Values With Other Executives' Instrumental Values

Instrumental Value	CEOs' Composite Rank	Senior Executives' Composite Rank[a]	Middle Managers' Composite Rank[a]	Supervisors' Composite Rank[a]
Honest	1	1	2	2
Responsible	2	2	1	1
Ambitious	3	6	8	7
Capable	4	3	3	3
Imaginative	5	4	4	5
Courageous	6	12	14	16
Broadminded	7	8	6	6
Logical	8	5	5	4
Independent	9	9	9	8
Loving	10	14	13	12
Self-controlled	10	7	7	10
Helpful	12	11	10	9
Intellectual	13	10	11	11
Forgiving	14	15	16	15
Cheerful	15	13	12	13
Polite	16	16	15	17
Clean	17	17	17	14
Obedient	18	18	18	18

a. Based on a national survey of American managers (Schmidt & Posner, 1982, p. 34).

plishment. His primary instrumental values (also in descending order) were: forgiving, honest, broadminded, capable, and responsible.

Robert indicated that his "upbringing had a lot to do" with the values he held most dear, but that he had reordered his values and his life somewhat due to the "down times" of the early 1990s. In particular, his Christian faith had become much more important to him in recent years, as indicated by his selection of two important Christian values as most dear to his heart: salvation and forgiveness.

Despite the high importance of Christian values in his life, Robert refrained from talking about his faith to others and wanted members of other faiths to feel comfortable working in his organization. He had a personal rule to speak about matters of faith to other employees only when asked directly about them. However, he was increasingly conscious of living consistently with his values as "that is the most powerful testimony and the least oppressive."

Randy Maxwell

The primary terminal values selected by Randy were: self-respect, sense of accomplishment, wisdom, exciting life, and happiness. His primary instrumental values to achieve these ends were: honest, courageous, imaginative, ambitious, and broadminded.

Randy indicated that his values were most influenced by his experience as a helicopter pilot in Vietnam. During his experience in Vietnam, he learned that imagining a positive outcome, being honest with his troops, and displaying courage under fire were the key ingredients to self-respect and successful accomplishment of the mission. Indeed, he credits these experiences with keeping him alive and giving him a "bit of wisdom" about life. Although he admitted that Vietnam was a very trying time for him, he would never trade the lessons he learned from that experience.

Randy expressed his values to the rest of his organization by trying to live and act consistently with them. Furthermore, he tried to build administrative systems and cultural norms in his organization that were consistent with his most deeply held values. For example, he developed an elaborate management by objectives system, which he hoped would stimulate extraordinary accomplishments and a sense of pride in his employees. Also, he encouraged workers to monitor themselves and just get the work done rather than "make a showing at work each day and fritter away time." He struggled with how to encourage individual initiative while stimulating teamwork but felt his firm "did a good job overall in this balancing act."

Richard Farr

The primary terminal values in Richard's life were: sense of accomplishment, family security, wisdom, self-respect, and happiness. His primary instrumental values were: honest, responsible, cheerful, self-controlled, and ambitious.

Richard indicated that his terminal values were most heavily influenced by the loss of his father when he was a teenager. This loss forced him to be very concerned about "being the man of the family" and accomplishing things and maintaining the family's security and being responsible and cheerful. In contrast, he speculated that his instrumental values were influenced by his mentors in the business world, who emphasized honesty and ambition.

Within his organization, Richard was quite task oriented and goal directed in his effort to reach his ambitious goals and create a new and vibrant banking company. He justified all the time and energy that he put into the job as "something that was fun and as a way to take care of my family." However, he worried about the future of his teenage sons, who increasingly rejected his authority and were experimenting with other values. Richard was a self-described "cheerful optimist" who demonstrated a "can-do" attitude constantly. He valued being in control at all times but admired people who were more spontaneous than himself. He acknowledged that his wife was his best friend, and she was the one with whom he was completely honest about his most vulnerable thoughts and feelings.

Steven Zolte

Steven's primary terminal values included: salvation, family security, self-respect, sense of accomplishment, and having an exciting life. His preferred instrumental values were: honest, capable, imaginative, responsible, and ambitious.

Steven surmised that his values came from his rather strict upbringing and from "being the oldest son." His Christian faith was also very important to him and clearly influenced his values and behavior. Steven's vigorous work ethic and strong moral framework manifested itself in his professional and personal life quite consistently.

Steven's Christian values guided his entire life at work and at home. He "saw the world in black and white" and lived according to what he saw as right and wrong. He asserted that he was rarely confused or in doubt about what was the right thing to do while leading his organization. He indicated that several members of his top management team were from the Jewish faith, but he did not feel that such rituals as his annual celebration of a company Christmas party made them feel uncomfortable or excluded. He emphasized behavior (rather than words) that stemmed from his Christian perspective and epitomized the Protestant work ethic.

Joseph Henderson

Joseph listed his primary terminal values as follows: salvation, wisdom, exciting life, self-respect, and sense of accomplishment. His list of prime instrumental values included honest, courageous, self-controlled, broadminded, and loving.

Joseph indicated that his life and values were established in childhood, but he got a "wake-up call" when he lost his job and his first marriage broke up. It was these traumatic events that caused him to clarify his values and live according to them. Notably, his faith was strengthened by these events, and he became "more intimate and aware of being a servant of God."

Joseph's Christianity also guided his values, but his faith was relatively abstract and nondogmatic. In particular, he viewed his faith as something to guide his own behavior, and he struggled constantly to turn his will over to God. He was quite tolerant of other faiths and value systems in his organization, but he would not tolerate behaviors that destroyed trust within and without the organization. Commenting on the pressures of the job and how his values help him, Joseph states,

> I'll tell you, it takes a lot of pressure off. I mean, I don't feel responsible totally for the results here. I do feel responsible for doing the best I can, but I am not driving this thing; and I don't want to drive it. I want to do the very best that I can and just see where that leads us.

Finally, within his top management team, he constantly states, "It is OK to make mistakes of the head, but it's not OK to make mistakes of the heart." According to him, this emphasis allows for true teamwork in his top management team.

Michael Breen

The top five terminal values for Michael were salvation, love, wisdom, happiness, and sense of accomplishment. The top five instrumental values for him were loving, forgiving, honest, responsible, and cheerful.

Michael indicates that he got most of his values from his mother's influence while growing up. However, his values and life shifted after witnessing the birth of his first child. During this singular experience, he came "to know the power and presence of God in my life and His all-pervasive love."

Michael's focus at work and at home was to live a life that followed Christ's example. He operationalized this as attempting to be as wise and loving as possible. Like Christ, he was detached from worldly concerns, even though he constantly faced the pressures of high Wall Street expectations each quarter and of extraordinary recent financial performance gains made at his bank. However, he avoided using traditional Christian words and rituals in his workplace "because that alienates people and prevents the message from being heard." His identity was firmly rooted in these values, but when he had a value conflict, he discussed the matter with a "minister friend" in another state. Overall, Michael's clear sense of values gave him a clarity and an energy that made him distinctive and quite charismatic.

Raymond Zuckerman

Raymond's primary terminal values were, in descending order, family security, happiness, self-respect, sense of accomplishment, and friendship. His primary instrumental values were honest, responsible, capable, helpful, and ambitious.

Raymond indicated that he came from a tightly knit family that wove his upbringing into their family business. In this situation, he learned that a focus on the family was paramount to maintaining it while dealing with the pressures of business. Raymond also liked to laugh and be playful at work and to be helpful to and caring about his workers. His life and family was inextricably tied into his family-owned firm, and this had a major influence on his values.

Summing Up

If a central activity of leaders is to clarify and instill shared organizational values, executives need to be clear about their own personal values and live according to them. In this chapter, we used Rokeach's (1973) typology of terminal and instrumental values to explore the value systems of CEOs. Terminal values are those preferences that we seek as ends in life, whereas instrumental values are those preferences that we seek as the guiding principles, or means, of life.

Based on the general survey, the top four terminal values of CEOs are a sense of accomplishment, family security, self-respect, and salvation. These terminal values are quite different from those of the general American public, but the differences may be due to the fact that the American public was surveyed 30 years earlier. Notably, the top four instrumental values of the CEOs were honest (by a large margin), responsible, ambitious, and capable. Interestingly, these values were quite consistent with the American public's top instrumental values as well as other executive values at other levels. Thus, the value priorities for instrumental values may reflect widely held American values that have not changed over time.

The seven CEOs who agreed to participate in field interviews were remarkably consistent in their terminal and instrumental values, as they tended to emphasize the same values as the general population of CEOs surveyed. Most of the CEOs who participated in the field study credited their upbringing and a life-changing event or series of events for their current values. In their work settings, they consistently argued that behavior was more compelling than words to reinforcing their values, but they discussed those values when questioned about them. All CEOs emphasized the importance of knowing and living your values as a key to success in life, not just the business world.

Individual Shadow Work With Personal Values

Hunter Lewis (1990) argues that personality and values are highly interrelated but distinct parts of what it means to be human. I believe that we can use knowledge about our personality to clarify what our values are and choose values that affirm life. To pursue this shadow work section, you must know something about your personality. In other words, knowledge about our personality can be useful to explore and develop our value systems.

Lewis (1990) argued that there are six ways to arrive at one's conscious values: (a) using our logic, (b) using our feelings, (c) deriving values from our senses, (d) intuiting our values, (e) basing our values on some authority, and (f) relying on science to inform us of our values. Interestingly, the first four ways correspond to the four ways of knowing discussed in Chapter 3 (i.e., thinking, feeling, sensing, and intuiting), and the last two ways are just specific applications of the first four. For example, if I feel good within a certain religious institution, I am more likely to follow its authority in the values for my life. Similarly, if science emphasizes logical conclusions and I am logically oriented, then I would probably rely on science to be the arbiter of my values. Consequently, we will focus on the first four ways of exploring our values.

When we value something, it goes into our conscious mind, and this value guides our choices in life. However, this also means that we devalue its opposite, and this opposite value resides in our unconscious mind, our shadow. Interestingly, our shadow often expresses itself in this devaluation process. For example, public "slips of tongue," mean-spirited gossip or jokes, extreme hate of our enemies, driven attempts to avoid certain things, and dreams about what we devalue offer clues to where our shadow work must begin (Zweig & Wolf, 1997).

When there is a difference between what we believe to be our most precious values and what values actually guide our behavior, our shadow is in control; and we have shadow work to explore. There are various names for this discrepancy. For example, George England (1967) distinguishes between "intended" and "operative" values. Chris Argyris (1982) distinguishes between "espoused" values and values "in use." And Abraham Zaleznick (1997) talks about "symbolic" and "real" values. For the purposes of this book, I have referred to these two sets of values as our public values and our private values. When you notice a gap between your public and private values, there is a need to reconcile these differences. The four approaches identified by Lewis (1990) and discussed below can be helpful, especially if you pursue the shadowy path for yourself.

1. *Logical approach—Natural path for thinking types, shadowy path for feeling types.* Value systems based on logic try to reinforce clear linkages between cause and effect. The causes and effects and linkages are catalogued into distinct categories, and communication tends to be quite linear. Testing the logic, particularly through deductive thinking,

is fundamental to this way of knowing your values. The Rokeach (1973) Value Survey is a particularly useful means for exploring this approach. Fill out this survey and identify your value priorities.

2. *Emotional approach—Natural path for feeling types, shadowy path for thinking types.* This path focuses on common ground with certain groups (e.g., family, work group, racial group, socioeconomic class, or nation) and opposition to other groups (e.g., enemies). Values are fostered that reinforce the identity of the "in" group and disavows the "out" group. Identify your preferred groups and the groups you disdain. Examine the emotional stimulus that operates when you are close to those disdained groups. Explore that disdain.

3. *Sense experience approach—Natural path for sensing types, shadowy path for intuitive types.* This path avoids abstraction and seeks verification in the five senses. If you cannot arrive at the value through your hearing, seeing, touching, smelling, or tasting, then it is not to be trusted. It is highly practical in its emphasis on personal experience, but it does not lend itself to categorization or communication very easily because personal experiences vary from person to person. Identify some personal experiences that lead to your deepest values.

4. *Intuiting approach—Natural path for intuitive types, shadowy path for sensing types.* The intuitive path is a nonverbal and highly abstract path using your "sixth" sense. Ideas and values come at unexpected times in surprising ways. However, once an intuitive insight is translated into words, it starts sounding like the other paths. Therefore, this path does not lend itself to description or communication as easily as the other three paths (Lewis, 1990). Meditate quietly and regularly on what your values are and let the insights come "naturally" to you.

5

Spirituality of Executive Leaders

Most of us have jobs that are too small for our spirits.
— Studs Terkel, 1974, p. 484

*The most important things in life should be first God, then family,
then work.*
— J. Peter Grace, CEO, W. R. Grace & Company
1985 Annual Report

*The Wall Street Journal accused Henry Ford of "economic blunders
if not crimes" which would soon return to plague him and the
industry he represents as well as organized society. In a naive wish
for social improvement, declared the newspaper, Ford had injected
"spiritual principles into a field where they do not belong"—a heinous
crime. Captains of industry lined up to condemn "the most foolish
thing ever attempted in the industrial world."*
— James Collins & Jerry Porras, 1994, p. 53

Spirituality is the third, and perhaps most elusive, aspect of executive
character. According to William Eichman (1990), a teacher at State
College, Pennsylvania, "If you take spiritual practice seriously you will
be confronted by your dark side. This is an axiom. The spiritual quest
is dangerous. Seeking truth means experiencing pain and darkness, as

well as the clear white light" (p. 134). However, David Steindl-Rast (1990), a Benedictine monk, maintains that the dominant spiritual path for most Americans, namely Christianity, has not done particularly well at cultivating a practical method for integrating the shadow.

Spirituality can and often does involve formal religious practices, but some individuals, particularly baby boomers, are shunning religious institutions in favor of a more personal path (Roof, 1993; Wuthnow, 1988; Yankelovich, 1981). Because spirituality is a more encompassing term than religiosity, we will focus on the larger context. However, religion is a central part of life for many people, and that aspect of spirituality will also be considered here.

Spirituality is about living the great questions of life, as opposed to finding answers (Rutte, 1996). In a survey of business executives, Gilbert Fairholm (1996) reported that the following beliefs are characteristic of executive spirituality: (a) there is a higher, more intelligent force; (b) the essence of self separates humans from creatures; and (c) spirituality is a source of comfort, strength, and happiness. Spirituality is a personal and complex part of our character that has been neglected for too long in business thought and practice (Conger, 1994; Fairholm, 1996; Fox, 1995; Novak, 1996). We explore the spirituality of executives in this chapter, and I offer some ideas for pursuing the spiritual journey in the workplace in the shadow work section.

Business and Spirituality

There has been a proliferation of interest in spirituality from the business world in the last decade. Business executives have historically gravitated to religious and spiritual matters in their private lives, but it was not until the 1990s that a person's spirituality could be discussed and/or practiced publicly at work (Kantrowitz, 1994). According to some, "Spirituality is an essential part of every one of us, but it isn't something companies traditionally have allowed employees to express at work. That is changing" (Laabs, 1995, p. 61).

The signs of spiritual expressions are everywhere throughout corporate America. For example, there are now 4,000 chaplains who work for private corporations (excluding hospitals, jails, and colleges), and demand is growing dramatically ("Chaplains in the Workplace," 1997). Increasing numbers of companies are offering sanctuaries for introspec-

Exhibit 5.1 Popular Spirituality in the Workplace Books

Author(s)	Year Published	Title	Publisher
✓ Covey	1989	*7 Habits of Highly Effective People*	Simon & Schuster
Needleman	1991	*Money and the Meaning of Life*	Doubleday Books
Roskind	1992	*In the Spirit of Business*	Celestial Arts
Renesch	1992	*New Traditions in Business*	Berrett-Koehler
Ray & Rinzler	1993	*The New Paradigm in Business*	Putnam
Chappel	1993	*The Soul of a Business*	Bantam
Hawley	1993	*Reawakening the Spirit in Work*	Berrett-Koehler
Autry	1994	*Life and Work*	William Morrow
Whyte	1994	*The Heart Aroused*	Doubleday
✓ Conger (ed.)	1994	*Spirit at Work*	Jossey-Bass
Nair	1994	*A Higher Standard of Leadership*	Berrett-Koehler
Fox	1995	*The Reinvention of Work*	Harper Collins
Bolman & Deal	1995	*Leading With Soul*	Jossey-Bass
Jones	1995	*Jesus—CEO*	Hyperion
Briner	1996	*The Management Methods of Jesus*	Thomas Nelson
Novak	1996	*Business as a Calling*	Free Press
Jaworski	1996	*Synchronicity*	Berrett-Koehler
Fairholm	1997	*Capturing the Heart of Leadership*	Praeger
Shipka	1997	*Leadership in a Challenging World*	Butterworth-Heineman

tion, prayer rooms, and contemplation gardens (Galen, 1995; Laabs, 1995). Conferences on spirituality in the workplace are being offered on an almost monthly basis (e.g., The Center for Visionary Leadership and its annual Spirituality at Work Conference). Even consultants now specialize in assisting corporations to move spirituality more consciously and sensitively into the workplace (e.g., Rutte, 1996). Creating community and caring for the employee's soul is front and center for many organizations today (Mirvis, 1997).

However, the clearest sign of spirituality becoming more public and acceptable in corporate America is the growing number of books on the subject. On this front, there has been an explosion. Exhibit 5.1 identifies some of the more popular books, but this is by no means an exhaustive list.

Executive Religiosity

America is the most religiously oriented country of all the developed nations (Van Buren, 1996). For example, 9 of every 10 Americans report that they pray regularly, and this activity has not diminished over the last four decades (Gallup Report, 1987). Furthermore, more than 6 of 10 Americans claim that religion is very important in their lives, and more than 4 of every 10 attend church regularly (Barna, 1994). Also, America is predominantly an orthodox Judeo-Christian nation where 2 of 3 Americans affiliate with this religious perspective (Barna, 1994).

Given the high rate of religiosity in this country, one would expect religion to play some role in CEOs' lives. In fact, CEOs are even more religiously inclined than the general public. For example, in a survey of the 100 largest firms, 65% of CEOs said they regularly attend church, as compared to the national average of 42% (Kallen, 1986). Similarly, in a sample of a broader array of firms, it was reported that more than 80% of CEOs described themselves as *somewhat* or *very* religious (Kurtz, Boone, & Fleenor, 1989).

Despite this high rate of religiosity, CEOs have been criticized for their lack of religious integrity in their business behavior (Kallen, 1986). Some blame CEOs for separating their religious ideals from their workplace practices (Torbert, 1996). Other observers argue that too often executive leaders operate with the motto: "The business of business is business," which is commonly translated to mean that religious ideals do not belong and are not practical in the business world (Fairholm, 1997).

Others blame failures on the part of religious institutions for this separation (Vaill, 1996b). For example, Matthew Fox, a former Dominican priest who was removed from the Roman Catholic church for his controversial views, states,

If you teach people that the number one problem is their sin and that when they came into the world they made a blotch on existence, they'll never get over it. This is religious abuse. We need to completely rethink religion in America. (Novick & Brown, 1995, p. 9)

Other observers are a bit more benign in their criticism of American religion, pointing out that Americans use religion "therapeutically" to feel better after they make decisions rather than to guide their decision-making process (Van Buren, 1996).

Regardless of the reason for the lack of religious consistency in the business world, spirituality is ultimately transformative, and some very religious CEOs are not transformed by their religious commitments (Torbert, 1996). Consequently, we must be careful in interpreting the outward signs of religious affiliation as indicators of spiritual renewal in the executive wing.

Religious Affiliations of CEOs

Nonetheless, it is interesting and useful to explore the religious orientations of CEOs, because the very roots of the capitalistic system grew out of the Protestant work ethic (Weber, 1920/1958). For example, Burck (1976) reported that Episcopalians, Presbyterians, and Method-ists were 11% of the national population but 50% of the CEO population during the 1970s. In contrast, Roman Catholics were 22% of the national population but only 14% of the CEO population; and Baptists were 14% of the national population and 3% of the CEO population. However, in a more recent national survey, Kurtz et al. (1989) reported that the overrepresentation of Episcopalians and Presbyterians was diminish-ing over time and that the CEO population was more and more begin-ning to look like the rest of America in terms of religious commitment.

Exhibit 5.2 specifically illustrates the trend toward a more repre-sentative array of religions adopted by CEOs. For example, at the turn of the century, 38% of CEOs were Episcopalian; that proportion has steadily decreased to 17% in 1989. In contrast, the proportion of CEOs who follow the Roman Catholic faith has grown over the century from 7% to 15%—still less than the national average of 19% but much closer to the general population (Barna, 1994). In sum, over the last century, CEOs have increasingly pursued a more diverse religious path that looks more like the rest of America.

Also, previous studies have indicated industry and regional influ-ences of CEO religious practices. For example, Kurtz et al. (1989) found

Exhibit 5.2 National Trends in Religious Denominations of CEOs

Religious Denomination	1900[a]	1950[a]	1976[a]	1989[b]
Episcopalian	38%	30%	21%	17%
Presbyterian	17%	23%	20%	16%
Methodist	12%	10%	9%	7%
Roman Catholic	7%	9%	14%	15%
Congregational	8%	7%	8%	3%
Baptist	2%	6%	3%	5%
Jewish	3%	5%	6%	6%
Lutheran	1%	3%	4%	5%
Other	12%	7%	15%	22%
	100%	100%	100%	100%

a. From Burck (1976).
b. From Kurtz, Boone, & Fleenor (1989).

that CEOs in the utility and medical products industries tended to be more religiously committed, whereas CEOs in service industries were often less religiously inclined. Also, southerners appear to be the most committed to their religious faith, whereas people from the western part of the country are often the least committed to their religious tradition (Barna, 1994).

Finally, religious executives are more apt to behave differently than nonreligious executives, according to several studies. For example, Kurtz et al. (1989) found that religious executives were more likely to have a sense of humor, preferred more structured work, and were better adjusted psychologically than nonreligious executives.

Of the 91 CEOs who responded to my regional survey, 84 (92.3%) affiliated with the Christian tradition, 3 were Jewish, 1 was connected to the Islamic faith, and 3 indicated no affiliation. Clearly, the CEOs in this study were largely (more than 95%) from the Judeo-Christian tradition.

However, there was a proliferation of denominational expressions among this group of respondents. Exhibit 5.3 reveals that most of the CEOs were from the Methodist, Presbyterian, and Episcopalian traditions, consistent with religious affiliation preferences indicated in the past. However, these three denominations accounted for fewer than

Exhibit 5.3   Religious Denominations of CEOs and Current National
Statistics

Rank	Religious Denomination	Number of CEOs	Study Proportion	National Proportion[a]
1	Methodist	22	24.1%	5.1%
2	Presbyterian	13	14.3%	1.6%
3	Episcopalian	10	11.0%	0.9%
4	Baptist	8	8.8%	13.8%
5	Roman Catholic	7	7.7%	22.7%
6	Lutheran	5	5.5%	3.1%
7	Church of Christ	3	3.3%	0.6%
7	Jewish	3	3.3%	1.6%
9	Unity	2	2.2%	0.1%
10	Islam	1	1.1%	1.9%
10	Church of God	1	1.1%	0.1%
10	Mormon	1	1.1%	1.8%
10	Evangelical	1	1.1%	1.7%
10	Nondenominational	1	1.1%	
	Other/unknown/unaffiliated	17	18.7%	45.0%
		91	100.0%	100.0%

a. From the *Yearbook of American & Canadian Churches* (1997).

50% of the CEOs surveyed. The remaining CEOs were affiliated with
11 other religious denominations, mostly within the Judeo-Christian
tradition.

Religious Orientations of CEOs

To examine some of the motivation behind this religious expression,
the CEOs also filled out Allport and Ross's (1967) Religious Orientation
Scale (ROS), the most frequently used measure of religiosity (Donahue,
1985). The ROS was developed to determine the motivation behind
religious commitment. Extrinsically motivated individuals are ones
who are motivated by getting some material benefit for themselves. It
is the religion of comfort and social convention, a self-serving instrumental approach shaped to suit oneself. Intrinsically motivated indi-

Exhibit 5.4 Religious Orientation of CEOs

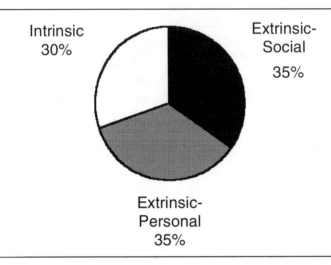

Intrinsic
30%

Extrinsic-
Social
35%

Extrinsic-
Personal
35%

viduals are ones who are motivated by some inner connection to a higher power. It is the religion of meaning, and it provides a framework for a person's overall life. This scale has been extensively tested over several decades of research and has been found to be reliable and valid after slight refinements to the questions are made (Donahue, 1985; Leong & Zachar, 1990). These refinements were made to the scale, and the instrument was included with other items in our overall survey.

Exhibit 5.4 has the results of our CEOs' responses to the refined ROS 14-item scale. As can be seen from this exhibit, nearly two thirds of the CEOs are involved with religion for extrinsic reasons, whereas only one third are involved for intrinsic reasons. Therefore, the extrinsic scale was further subdivided into personal and social subfactors. Previous theory and research have shown that extrinsic motivation typically comes in one of two forms (Allport & Ross, 1967). The extrinsic-personal form is when individuals engage with religion to advance some worldly desire (e.g., "I pray mainly to gain relief and protection"). The extrinsic-social form is when individuals engage with religion simply to be with other people in a religious setting (e.g., "I go to church mostly to spend time with my friends"). Interestingly, the CEOs are almost evenly split between each of the three classical motivations (i.e., intrinsic, personal, and social) for engaging with religion.

Exhibit 5.5 CEOs' Self-Reported Degree of Religious/Spiritual
Experiences

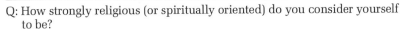

Q: How strongly religious (or spiritually oriented) do you consider yourself
to be?

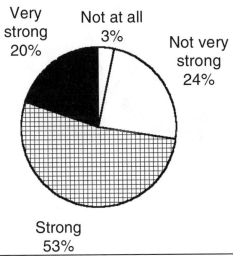

Spiritual Experiences of CEOs

In an effort to learn more about executive spirituality, we also asked
the CEOs about their spiritual experiences and practices. A recent but
promising scale developed in the medical community was used to
examine the CEOs' spiritual experiences. This six-item scale was developed by Kass, Friedman, Leserman, Zuttermeister, and Benson
(1991); and it is called the "Inspirit" scale of spiritual experience. It has
strong reliability and validity within a Judeo-Christian setting and has
been shown to be positively correlated with intrinsic religiosity ($r =$
.69) and with numerous positive health outcomes. Because of the heavy
concentration of Judeo-Christians in our survey population, the spiritual "assumptions" in these survey items should not be problematic.

In Exhibit 5.5, a pie chart shows the distribution of responses to
the question dealing with how strongly religious or spiritual the CEOs
consider themselves to be. Notably, nearly three quarters of the respondents (73%) indicate that they consider themselves to be strongly reli-
gious/spiritual. In contrast, only 3% of the CEOs indicate they are not

Exhibit 5.6 CEOs' Self-Reported Spiritual Practices Frequency

Q: About how often do you engage in religious or spiritual practices?

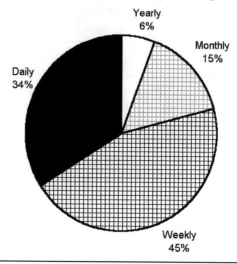

at all religious or spiritually inclined. Clearly, matters of religion and the spirit are important to chief executives.

The second question about the spiritual life of CEOs was concerned with how frequently they invest in spiritual disciplines or practices. Exhibit 5.6 reveals that nearly half (45%) of the responding CEOs indicated that they engage in some spiritual practice on a weekly basis. More than one third (34%) of the CEOs indicated that they engage in a daily spiritual practice. Clearly, CEOs invest time and energy in their spiritual life. Also, 15% of the CEOs engage in a monthly spiritual practice, and 6% of the CEOs are involved with their spiritual practice on an annual basis.

The third question dealing with spiritual experiences asked CEOs how often they feel close to some powerful spiritual force that seems to lift one outside of oneself (see Exhibit 5.7). More than one third of the CEOs (34%) indicated that this has never happened to them. Roughly one quarter (23%) indicated that this has happened once or twice in their lifetime. Interestingly, 30% of the CEOs indicated that this has happened to them several times in their lifetimes, and 8% indicated that this has happened to them often.

Exhibit 5.7   CEOs' Self-Reported Spiritual Connection Frequency

Q: How often have you felt as though you were very close to a powerful spiritual force that seemed to lift you outside of yourself?

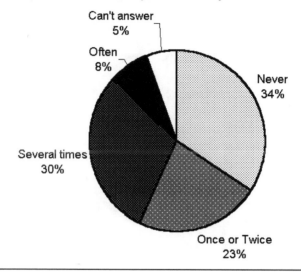

The fourth question asked the CEOs how close they felt to God (refer to Exhibit 5.8). The overwhelming majority (61%) indicated that they felt *somewhat close.* One of every five CEOs (20%) indicated that they did not feel very close to God at all. One in seven CEOs (14%) evaluated their relationship with God to be *extremely close* and only one respondent indicated that he does not believe in God.

The fifth spiritual experience question focused on whether or not the CEO had ever had a personal experience that convinced him that God exists. These responses are depicted in Exhibit 5.9. Nearly two thirds of the respondents (64%) indicated they had had a personal experience with God. Also, roughly one of every four respondents (24%) indicated that they have never had such an experience. Finally, 12% of the respondents indicated that they could not answer such a question.

Clearly, a person's conception of God influences the nature and quality of that same person's spiritual experiences. Therefore, the sixth and final question about their spiritual experiences was concerned with their conception of God. The CEOs were asked to indicate whether or

Exhibit 5.8 CEOs' Self-Reported Closeness to God

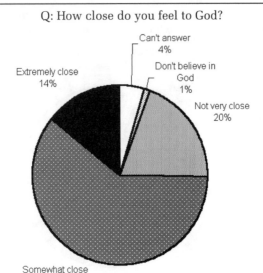

Q: How close do you feel to God?

Can't answer
4%

Don't believe in
God
1%

Extremely close
14%

Not very close
20%

Somewhat close
61%

Exhibit 5.9 CEOs' Self-Reported Personal Experience of God

Q: Have you ever had an experience that has convinced you that God exists?

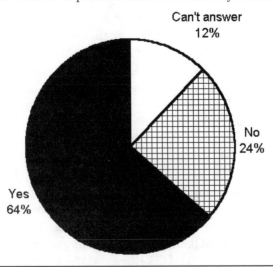

Can't answer
12%

No
24%

Yes
64%

Exhibit 5.10 CEOs' Self-Reported Conception of God

Q: Indicate whether you agree with this statement: "God dwells within you."

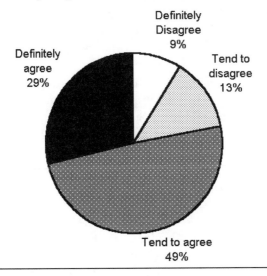

Definitely
Disagree
9%

Definitely
agree
29%

Tend to
disagree
13%

Tend to agree
49%

not they agreed with the statement that "God dwells within you." According to Exhibit 5.10, nearly 8 in every 10 CEOs (78%) agreed with this statement. In contrast, 2 of every 10 CEOs (22%) disagreed with this statement to varying degrees.

Case Studies of CEO Spirituality

Robert Masters

Robert grew up in a rural community. He was the oldest of seven children, and his parents were "very religious and fundamentalist," to use Robert's words. All the children were required to go to church all day Sunday and Wednesday evenings. According to Robert,

It is interesting how different members of the family reacted to that situation. I pretty much did what was expected of me. I sang in the choir and I became comfortable praying in public at a fairly early age. I was president of the Sunday night youth group for a couple of years before I went to college, and these are all the things that my parents wanted me to do. In contrast, my brothers rebelled against the church early on and refused to do any of it. It really was after college before I decided that I didn't want any of it, and there was a period of time in my twenties when I refused to go to church.

But after a few years, Robert had children of his own; his interest in faith and God was slowly rekindled. He took his children to Sunday school, and he began attending Sunday services at a local Church of Christ, a nondenominational Protestant church. However, in the mid-1980s, he wanted to "make a difference," so he started teaching Bible school classes and soon became president of the school. This then led to becoming a deacon in the church. However, as his faith grew, he began to realize that "things aren't as black and white as my parents and early interpretations of the Bible led me to believe." This became a theme in his teachings and leadership within the church. Soon, Robert was chairman of the church board and leader of a 10-person missionary committee. Next, he was in charge of an expansion committee that built an entirely new place of worship. In short, Robert found a way to use his talents as a manager within the church hierarchy, and this was very satisfying and meaningful to him.

Meanwhile, Robert's spiritual journey was enjoying new twists and turns in his professional life. You may recall that Robert was demoted from the CEO position, and soon the firm was in bankruptcy as a result of actions by his successor. According to Robert, "Prayer and my relationship with God is about the only thing that got me through that crazy time."

Furthermore, in 1992, Robert's father died quickly and unexpectedly of a heart attack. This event, coupled with his mounting work stress, changed his perspective on life dramatically. One of the biggest changes was in his prayer life and his relationship with God. He stated,

Most people pray to God to get things and that was the way I used to be. However, I have learned that after you have done everything humanly possible, you often need to turn it over to God and just say—"Thy will be done" and get on with it.

Indeed, just before the bankruptcy announcement, Robert humbly asked his prayer group at church to pray to God to give him "guidance and strength," which has become his daily prayer.

Soon after this "letting go" by Robert, several "unexplainable coincidences" started to occur. First, he connected with an investment banker involved with the bankruptcy in terms of a shared interest in serving children from poor families. Together, they developed a profit-sharing plan in the company, where half of excess profits would go to the employees and the other half would go to needy children. Next, he assembled a new board based on "complementary spiritual perspectives" and that has led to an unusually high-functioning governance team. Recently, new ideas come to him during ordinary times of the day (e.g., while shaving) that solve seemingly intractable problems. Robert credits all these developments to God's presence in his life.

Notably, Robert is enjoying life more now. His employees now bring religious and spiritual concerns to him in his office even though he is careful not to proselytize employees. He finds this turn of events deeply rewarding. He laughs more easily and celebrates "the small things in life" more. And Robert is convinced that the power of prayer by his prayer group was instrumental in the resurrection of his firm. Overall, Robert's religious orientation is highly intrinsic, as we can see from his life and from his survey responses.

Randy Maxwell

Randy attended church as a young boy growing up but commented that "it really didn't mean much to me." Randy's spiritual journey began in earnest during his tour of duty as a helicopter pilot in the Vietnam War. He emphasizes the importance of taking responsibility for oneself and working with God rather than pleading your case before God in times of trouble. Illustrating an approach that he admired was a Catholic chaplain with whom he served:

> He was a stereotypical (Irish-Catholic) Father O'Shea from the Boston area. He was in his mid-thirties, I believe. This chaplain had a strong faith and loved to serve and be with the troops. He made a difference. I was particularly struck by his behavior when he would drive to various hot spots. He'd put on his flack

jacket and helmet. Then he would put the "chicken plate" underneath the seat and sandbag the bottom of the Jeep to protect it from mines. He'd put his .45 on and carry an M-16. And we would tease him and say something like, "Doesn't look like you have too much faith today, Father." And he would laugh and say back, "You know, when I need the Lord, He may just be a little busier with somebody else; and I may have to take care of myself for a few seconds." That thought and behavior made sense to me.

Randy returned to the church after his children were born. He and his wife joined a Presbyterian church, but he was quite ecumenical in his outlook. Reflecting on his view of religion, he stated,

> I've got kids and just like lots of other baby-boomer yuppies, I reasoned, "Well, I'm not going to beat the Bible into them the way it was beaten into me, but I do want them to have a religious experience growing up." So we went back to the Presbyterian Church. I hate Bible thumping, but there is a need to put a structure around things, maybe put a name on some of this stuff we call life. I guess I am convinced that one can do it as a Presbyterian and one could do it as a Zen Buddhist. There are lots of different ways to get to Amarillo—bus, train, boat, whatever.

Randy's spiritual journey now is highly influenced by a connection with nature. He stated,

> Sometimes I get up early in the morning and go for a walk under the stars. Lately, I've been thinking that we spend so much energy getting BMWs and houses and even raising kids, but in 250 years from now, who is going to care? Strangely, that thought and time with the stars is comforting to me.

When asked how his spiritual journey influences his role as CEO, Randy declares that it has raised the importance of an informal but absolute concern for ethical conduct in the workplace. He argues that "ethics can't be established by policies and procedures; however, they are too important to be ignored." So he believes that it is incumbent on him to speak the truth and behave ethically "because I set the ethical tone in this organization."

Also, he believes that his spiritual journey gives him unique insights into what motivates himself and others. He points out that enthusiasm is literally translated as "filled with the spirit." Consequently, he tries to be enthusiastic about the company, and he seeks to cultivate the enthusiasm of his employees. He notes that paychecks can only take you so far: "Eventually you must tap into your spirit if you want some magic to happen."

Furthermore, he reasons that his spirituality helped him with the paradoxes of life. For instance, he believes that 200 years from now, the things that most of us worry about will not matter very much. However, he does believe that we are called to be good stewards of our time and talents. So he focuses on excellence day by day but does not take it too seriously if things do not work out all right.

In his private life, Randy tithes at his church even though his religious motivation was primarily extrinsic and social, according to his survey responses. He admits to praying spontaneously with such prayers as "I am the luckiest person alive, thank you." He is convinced that confronting death in Vietnam forced him to examine his mortality at an early age. Eventually, he accepted his mortality, and that has shifted his approach to life ever since. He firmly states, "Now I don't want to die. The difference is, I am no longer afraid of death. It is just that I have a lot I want to do before I leave this earth."

Richard Farr

Richard was currently attending a Methodist church, but he admitted to not being very involved with the church. According to him, "I am wandering around when it comes to church homes." Feeling a need to explain this statement, he stated,

I was born a Baptist, but to me, it is what is in your heart that counts. When I was very young, my father died. After that, I kind of drifted completely away from the church. Then in junior high, I started going to the Episcopalian church because my best friend attended that one. Then, in high school, I changed best friends and became a Lutheran like him once again. His father was a Lutheran minister, and he became almost like a surrogate father to me. I spent almost as much time at their home as my own! Because of this fondness for this family, I went to a Lutheran school and met my wife, who was a strong Lutheran herself. Soon we were married. We then moved around—first to Florida, then to South Carolina, and then to Tennessee. There aren't many Lutheran churches in Tennessee, but the particular church really doesn't matter to me anyway. So we looked around and ended up at a Methodist church. There are some theological differences, but they don't amount to much in my opinion.

Commenting on his spiritual practices, Richard indicated that he is not a very demonstrative person, so his spirituality is a fairly private matter. He stated, "I think it's more the way you live your life rather than emotional demonstrations of faith in public." He believes that "if you do the right things for the right reasons, God will give you the alternatives and give you the wisdom to make the right choices."

Richard prays each morning. He prays because it "calms and relaxes" him. His most common prayer is for wisdom. Laughing, he recounted the following story:

Basically, I pray each day as I drive to work. After about a week of following this habit, I went speeding down the highway and got pulled over and received a speeding ticket. After the officer left me, I looked skyward and said, "God, how can you let me get a speeding ticket when I am talking with you?" He sure does have a surprising way of responding to our prayers now, doesn't He?

Richard uses his faith to get him through the tough times in life as well as to give him guidance. He mentioned that it was particularly helpful after being fired previously in his career. He recounts,

I was fired once—everybody has to go through that sometime. I felt pretty low, but I went to Sunday school a couple of days later anyway. At that school, a close friend of mine was teaching a big class of 150 people or so. I don't remember what he said, but I do remember that he forcefully quoted a passage from Psalms in the Bible. And I remember leaving Sunday school and going to the sanctuary, and I read the passage from Psalms that he quoted. I can't explain it but something just clicked. It felt like God was speaking to me to get my head screwed on right and to jump back into the fray. It calmed me and energized me at the same time. It was a spiritual experience that I will never forget.

Richard started trusting God when he realized that he could not do some things on his own. This was described as a gradual process that was speeded up by becoming a husband and soon thereafter becoming a father of two sons. Now his marriage is well-established, and his sons are teenagers. Describing this evolution, he stated,

You know, at the ripe old age of 21, you think you don't need help. My 21-year-old son thinks that he can conquer everything. And I want him to have confidence, but he is going down fool's hill with that attitude. I just hope that he doesn't make too many mistakes. I was like him when I was his age, but slowly I learned that there are definite limits to my knowledge and power. I don't like it, but I need help. Ultimately, being a husband and father has taught me about faith more than my work has. However, those lessons are definitely carried over to my work.

Consistent with Richard's earlier comments, he is extrinsically motivated to attend church for personal reasons. Prayer was his primary avenue of faith, and his family is his primary "sanctuary" of worship and learning.

Steven Zolte

Steven's spiritual journey began in a stormy fashion. According to him, "My father was a Catholic and my mother was a Baptist. Their religious beliefs mixed like oil and water." This unlikely combination of religious outlooks was played out in Steve's early religious life as well. He attended Catholic Mass with his father and went to Catholic schools until the fifth grade, but he also attended Baptist services with his mother. Because his parents were not getting along well, they speculated that maybe religion held the answer. So Steven's mother began attending an Episcopalian church and indeed joined the church shortly thereafter. Regrettably, Steven's parents were unable to reconcile their differences; they divorced when he was 10 years old.

At age 11, Steven left Catholic schools and started attending the Episcopal church with his mother. In addition, he started attending the Episcopalian school from sixth until eighth grade. He was soon very involved in the church; he became confirmed and eventually became an acolyte. He would spend his entire Sunday at church as that was where all his friends were.

At age 13, Steven's mother remarried, and he now had a stepfather. According to Steven,

> By the time I was 13, I was really on my own. I carried my own weight. I was a very mature kid. My mother was working; my stepfather worked; they were trying to make ends meet. I was the oldest, and I was often responsible for my younger sister. There was a lot going on. What kept me going when things really got crazy was attending church and praying regularly. Back then, they left the church open 24 hours a day, seven days a week. Sometimes I would go to the church, go up to the altar and pray. I felt like I got a lot of help. I clearly felt the presence of God, and I felt like I had some special help that maybe other people didn't get.

In his 20s, Steven became disenchanted with the Episcopal church—it no longer fit with his values. When he was 24, he married a woman who was active in the Baptist church. He started attending Baptist services and when he was 33, he joined the Baptist Church, where he was baptized by total immersion. Steven recounted the following reasons for switching his church affiliation: "I am pretty much a black and white guy. Life is fairly simple for me. It is either right or it isn't. The Baptist Church takes this same approach and that appeals to my way of things."

When asked if he differentiates between his religious and spiritual lives, Steven declared,

> They are one in the same for me. You go to a church that teaches what you believe, and it is spiritual in nature. To me, they ought

to be one in the same. If they are not, there is something probably wrong with the church and you need to go elsewhere.

Prayer is the center of Steven's spiritual life. He studies the Bible, but his prayer time is his "most meaningful time."

When asked how his spiritual life affects his role as CEO, Steven mentioned that, first, it enables him to be clear about what his priorities in life are: Faith is first, family is second, and work is third. Then, he strives to live his life consistent with those priorities. For example, he never schedules meetings on Saturday or Sunday as he believes that is a time for family and church. Second, he tries to lead by example and let that speak for his values and beliefs. His firm does not tolerate dishonesty or sexual harassment. According to Steven, "I've had six managers with more than 20 years of experience each who didn't understand our zero-tolerance policy, and they are gone." Similarly, Steven works very hard and expects others to do so as well.

Consistent with the earlier discussion, Steven appears to be intrinsically motivated on the ROS. In sum, religion and the spiritual life are very important, well defined, and integral to his role as CEO.

Joseph Henderson

Joseph grew up in a traditional home with two churchgoing Christian parents and a couple of younger brothers. His mother always insisted on her sons attending church each Sunday and, to Joseph, this made sense. But his younger brothers resisted. In Joseph's own words,

> I became a Christian at a very young age, and I always had a vital relationship with Him. I didn't ever consider myself religious or spiritual, but I had an ongoing relationship with God and a sense of trying—of understanding, that there was a God and He was interested in my life. I needed to understand what that was and to stay in as close touch with Him that I could. However, my brothers didn't see things the same way I did, and they avoided church.

Joseph experienced considerable success at an early age. By his early 30s, he became a senior vice president of a multibillion-dollar company. In addition to his power and considerable income, he was happily married and raising healthy children. Joseph's health was excellent, and his outlook on the future was optimistic.

However, things suddenly changed when he was in his mid-40s:

> I am convinced that the Lord, in effect, booted me out of where I was because I wouldn't have let go on my own. While I never moved away from that relationship with God, I think I became less dependent on Him, more focused on my own ability to make things happen and so forth, and was flying pretty high, had made a fair amount of money, in a good position, and so forth. And I am so convinced what He did was to say, you know, "I'm going to pry you loose. Watch me." And so I ended up on the seat of my pants.

Caught in an internal "political battle," Joseph was dismissed from the company. Shortly thereafter, Joseph's wife of 25 years told him that she wanted a divorce, and this was granted (along with one half of all his assets). Distraught, Joseph reflected on this period with the following ideas:

> What this experience did was to put me in a position to say clearly to God: "I'm not in control. You are in control. You just put me where you want me, and I'll do my best." And once I reached that point, then He just began to create and make things happen. You see, I have learned that it is all about relationship. It has got nothing to do with things I must do, including going to church or even praying regularly. It's all about following His lead and staying in relationship with Him.

Initially, Joseph thought he would just go to work at some established company, building on his previous industry expertise. However, he felt a nudge within to start a new company. Reluctantly, Joseph followed this inner urge. He teamed up with three men who had "a common spiritual bond," and they launched an effort to start a new company. They met weekly to pray for the company and to pray for each other. They committed themselves as a team, "and when one guy stumbled, we agreed not to shoot him." It created an unusual top management team that outsiders had trouble understanding. For example, reporters from a well-known business magazine studied this team and asked, "Are you guys religious?" Joseph replied, "Well, I wouldn't say that. I'd just say that we all have a living relationship with God, and that kind of drives what we are doing."

When asked why Joseph avoids religious labels, he explains that religion and religious language alienate people, but a focus on God brings people together. Indeed, it is this common focus on God that Joseph credits for inspiring their business concept, for drawing the unique assembly of top management, and for gaining venture capital and bank credit.

Joseph is a practicing Baptist, but he emphasizes that the specific religion or religious practices are not what matter. On the ROS, Joseph was revealed to be intrinsically motivated.

Michael Breen

Michael recalls his spiritual journey beginning at the age of 6 or 7. His mother took him to a local Methodist church to hear a missionary tell his story about mission work for the church. For some unexplainable reason, Michael was affected deeply by this testimony:

> As this guy was telling his story, a light, a small light went off inside of me. I began to realize that this is an important part of who we are as people and that God is the creator and this is creation and that there really needs to be a relationship between the creator and creation. It really began as a sort of "aha" experience and then started to grow and evolve over the next 5 to 10 years. At the time, we were living in a small town in Indiana, and a lot of things revolved around the church.

In eighth grade, Michael's family moved to Cincinnati, and Michael lost all interest in learning more about this relationship between the creator and creation. This continued for the next 10 years or so until he witnessed the birth of his first child. According to Michael, this experience drew him back into his own childhood and made him remember what was most meaningful and relevant. And so he returned to matters of the spirit and faith. Michael recalls,

> I started to really pursue the spiritual journey again at that time. I believe that it was in my late 20s or so. In fact, I got so fired

up at that time that I actually concluded that I was going to leave this career as a banker and go to seminary to become a minister. My constant daily request was, "God I'm going to keep walking through these doors as long as they are open. If for some reason this is not what You want me to do, close a door for me and help me to recognize that the door is closed." And doors kept opening for me and I kept moving in new directions. And all of a sudden, a door closed. And it was a pretty loud bang, and it was pretty clear to me why it was closed. So I did not enter the seminary.

According to Michael, he did not have any "Damascus Road" experiences. It was more like ideas that grew from within himself, and with careful attention, he would gain new insights and direction. He explains, "it always seemed to start as a dim light and then slowly grow in intensity over time."

While this transformation was unfolding for Michael, his wife, a college professor, was becoming fearful. She liked their current life and did not want things to change much. But Michael was changing in many ways. Eventually, after a 5-year struggle, his wife concluded that their differences were irreconcilable, and she asked for a divorce. She left Michael after concluding that the changes he was undergoing were ruining their relationship and marriage. After a few years, Michael remarried a woman who was more aligned with his faith and journey.

According to Michael, religion and religious practices play a large role in his spiritual journey. He values the rituals of religion and makes them a centerpiece of his family life. His children attend Sunday school; they all worship together as a family; they pray regularly as a family; Michael and his wife even team teach classes at church. He stated, "The motto for our family is: Love the Lord first, love the family second, and this thing called work and play comes third."

Despite this religiosity, Michael describes his spirituality as "the umbrella that stands over all this activity." He believes that it is possible to be very religious, but not be spiritual at all. In fact, he is critical of many churches, his own included, for pushing God into the background and becoming an exclusive club. Michael believes that the key is "a living relationship with God."

Regarding his work, Michael views his spiritual walk to be central to his leadership roles in life. In his own words,

Well, the older I become, the more I believe that this whole world of leadership, of being a CEO, is really more a matter of the heart than it is a matter of the mind. When I was younger, I viewed leadership in an intellectual way. As I get older, I view it more of an emotional and more of a heartfelt way. Leadership is all about change—changing yourself so that others can change as well.

Michael is an unconventional leader of a bank, and his bank is doing unconventional things. According to him, he battles regularly with his board to make the necessary changes. Although the changes he is attempting are "exhausting and not without risk," he is not intimidated by the challenges. He stated,

I have a very strong sense of who I am and why I am a valuable human being. I don't base my sense of self-worth on a nice office; it doesn't come from being a leader of a corporation that does well financially. It doesn't come from accolades, because that can be there one day and gone the next. My sense of self-worth is that I am a creation of God. I never question that, so I can withstand a lot of criticism. Furthermore, I have learned to trust my intuition; and more often than not, it is dead right.

Michael's ROS reveals him to be intrinsically motivated. At the beginning of every day, Michael offers the prayer, "What do You want me to do today—be a bank president or do you have some other avenue for me?" So far, the answer he keeps receiving is "to continue his ministry in the business world."

Raymond Zuckerman

Raymond was born to Jewish parents but did not consider himself a very religious person. In fact, his parents raised him in a very ecumenical fashion by having him attend a Methodist preschool program. This was followed by Christian Bible school training during the summertime and by the encouragement of friendships outside the Jewish faith. However, he did attend synagogue during his youth as well (Reformed tradition). In Raymond's own words, "I try to be a good person; which, if you're a good Jew, you're a good person. If you're a good

Methodist, you're a good person. I mean, a good whatever is a good person!"

Raymond stressed the importance of the spiritual journey. He stated,

> You either move forward or backward; you never stand still. Not only do you have to keep going, you have to keep learning, testing, and trying new things and making mistakes. You never arrive. You never get to the end. When you do get to the end, you're dead!

Indeed, learning seemed to be the primary component of Raymond's spirituality. After nearly three decades of being CEO of a major retail firm, he stated the following lesson: "I have learned that I can always do more, be more productive, do better things to help more people; there's more to know than I know. Everyday you learn more and more about what you don't know."

Visiting Israel had a profound impact on Raymond—so much so that he has visited it over 20 times in his lifetime. In keeping with his ecumenical nature, he recalls that his best trip was when he went with five Jewish couples and five Christian couples—"Very revealing, many different perspectives," according to him. He found one particular incident especially moving:

> My wife and I have been involved with a school in Israel. It is called Girl's Town. It is a religious school. A family friend wanted to do something in my parents' memory, so he gave a lot of money to this particular school. Somehow they found out I was going to be in Israel for the first time, so they bugged me to death about visiting the place. Well, I decided to visit it after all. On the way there, I asked the Israeli tour guide if he had heard about this school. He said, "No, it's just a religious school. I don't support anything religious because it is the religious people who are ruining this country." But something happened to him and me when we went there. Later, he admitted, "You know, I really spoke too quickly because it is a wonderful school." I would have to agree with him.

Raymond went on to say that his numerous visits to Israel gave him a deeper appreciation for the richness and sacrifices that people have made for religion. He marvels at the Jewish people's ability to handle persecution and to keep the country together while being surrounding by so many enemies. He particularly admires the Israelis' ability to learn and to function with such diverse people and religious sects.

In addition to visits to Israel, Raymond has also been influenced by a recent prayer experience. He tells the following story:

> I went to synagogue to pray with my nephew. I didn't go for myself; I went to be with him—he is very Orthodox. So we went there, and I started praying. All of a sudden, I started getting some unusual feelings; so I kept it up. Eventually, I started praying for all sorts of people in need. Meanwhile, a friend of our family has a baby. That baby isn't doing too well—it was steadily losing weight since birth. The pediatrician told her that it is getting dangerous. So I include this baby in my prayers. Shortly after that prayer, she started on the road to recovery. . . . It is coincidental. You will never know if prayer made a difference or not. But when these things happen you have to pay attention to them. You want to buy your "insurance," I guess.

Another recent coincidence affected him deeply. Raymond was talking to a friend in a hotel lobby in London. The wife of this friend had just had a stroke, and he was very distraught. Raymond offered to put a note in the Western Wall in Jerusalem—a very sacred practice. When he got there, he put many notes all over the wall. As he says, "You know, maybe it works. Can you afford to not do it in case that it does?" Raymond laughingly concludes, "I am a very superstitious person."

While not a very religious person, Raymond seems to be gaining a deeper and deeper appreciation for his religion over time. Paradoxically, he remains open to and appreciative of other religions as well. On the ROS, Raymond's answers indicated he had an extrinsic-personal orientation. Overall, Raymond's Jewish heritage is always in the background, driving his behavior in the workplace and increasingly occupying his thoughts.

Summing Up

Spirituality is central to executive character. Most of the CEOs in this study were religiously inclined, and most come from a Judeo-Christian background. Although most CEOs are affiliated with Protestant denominations, CEOs' religious affiliations more and more approximate the American populace. The religious orientation of CEOs is predominantly extrinsic, which may explain why CEOs are criticized for separating the ideals of their religion from their work life.

In terms of spiritual experience, a surprising number of CEOs report intense and regular spiritual experiences. Furthermore, most CEOs believe in a "God within" concept. Prayer was by far the most common spiritual practice, and many CEOs differentiated between their spiritual and religious lives.

In the case studies, we observed that all seven CEOs refuse to believe that their religion is the one and only way to know God. All acknowledge the importance of prayer in their lives, but they vary in their emphasis on the importance of religion. Notably, each person had some sort of "trigger event" that deepened his faith. These trigger events varied, but all had dramatic impacts on the CEOs. Some CEOs had positive trigger events, such as the birth of a child. However, most were negative in the sense that there was some major loss and then their relationship to God became more real and important to them. All of the CEOs admit that they are not in control, God is. Although not passive by any means, they all acknowledge the importance of a responsive relationship with God.

Individual Shadow Work
With Executive Spirituality

If you choose to do shadow work with spirituality, the metaphor of a journey into a strange new land is appropriate. The following ideas were gleaned from a book by Peter Richardson (1996) entitled, *The Four Spiritualities*, if you would like to read further on this subject. If you are still in the process of exploring and identifying your personality type, I suggest you pursue your "natural" or preferred path. However, if you want to explore your shadow energies and further develop your character, I suggest you pursue your unnatural or "shadowy" path.

1. *The Journey of Unity—Natural path for NTs; shadowy path for SFs.* The quest for great organizing principles that bind life and nature into one unity is a central focus of this journey. The motivation for determining these organizing principles comes from the search for clarity, truth, and social justice. Mentors for this way include such people as the Buddha and, more recently, Buckminster Fuller. Words and symbols are paramount to this path in an effort to achieve competence and clarity of orientation. A place of personal retreat is particularly valuable to this path.

2. *The Journey of Devotion—Natural path for SFs; shadowy path for NTs.* This journey is the most tangible and specific of the four paths. Quite often, pilgrimages to holy places are moving and meaningful to those engaged with this journey. Sacred stories hold particular meaning to those who take up this path, especially myths and stories about heroes of faith. Spiritual growth is grounded in personal experience, especially the experience of simple things, such as lighting a candle. If finding God is the object of this journey, God is often a personal and approachable entity. Direct service to others is fundamental to this path, and mentors for this way include Mohammed and St. Francis.

3. *The Journey of Works—Natural path for STs; shadowy path for NFs.* This journey is practical and involves a lifetime of effort, a constant and responsible attention to leading an active and productive life. The concept of duty is quite important to those on this path, and the practice of direct activity is paramount. Abiding by the law, or covenant, or established social order is very important to travelers along this path, and righteous responsibility or stewardship is often the guiding light. There is a need for identity and authority on this path, and people on this path often see their work as the fulfillment of their spirituality. Mentors for this path include Moses and Confucius, and clear guidelines of right and wrong are essential.

4. *The Journey of Harmony—Natural path for NFs; shadowy path for STs.* This journey is the most adaptable and fluid of the four pathways. Filled with hope and idealism, this path often revolves around

mysticism, which often confirms the harmony of life in the world. Personal discovery and growth are key words to those who take this route. For those on this pathway, "heal thyself" is often the starting point for spiritual growth. The journey of harmony focuses intently on the processes of human relationships, social interaction, and communication. It is egalitarian and intimate. Mentors along the way include Rabinadranath Tagore, an educator and artist from India, and Jesus of Nazareth. Structured discipline is required for progress along this path including such activities as keeping a journal, practicing yoga, or performing Sufi dances.

PART III

Creative Fruits
of Executive Leaders

Creating a Vision of the Future

Begin with the end in mind.
— Steven Covey, 1989, p. 95

Where there is no vision, the people perish.
— Proverbs 29:18

Just because a company has a vision statement (or something like it) in no way guarantees that it will become a visionary company!
— James Collins and Jerry Porras, 1994, p. 201

Most leaders and leadership development experts agree that one of the most important contributions of a leader is to create or help create a vision that brings with it commitment to organizational excellence and directs change efforts. If the leader casts a dark shadow throughout the organization, this vision will not be seen nor will it be shared by others. However, when the leader is a beacon of light, the vision is clear and compelling to all who choose to look.

Notably, a general survey of 300 executives within America's largest firms revealed that 79% of the respondents believe that a clear and effective long-term vision is necessary for a firm's survival (Beach,

1993). In a recent survey of 463 companies by Bain & Co., vision statements ranked as the most popular of 25 commonly used management tools, with 94% of the companies polled reporting their use (Stuart, 1994).

Consultants argue that an effective organizational vision facilitates critical decisions and organizational behavior in a wide variety of areas (Barker, 1990). These areas include, but are not limited to (a) focusing executive succession decisions (McClenahen, 1991), (b) working with suppliers (Bertodo, 1991), (c) framing strategic alliances (Stiles, 1994), (d) selecting directors for the board (Breitenbach, 1989), and (e) guiding organizational change efforts (Miles, Coleman, & Creed, 1995). Ben Tregoe, a successful and enduring management consultant, maintains that the wrong strategic vision is worse than inefficiency because it leads to unproductive results (Heller, 1990). And Ian Wilson (1992) argues that nothing sets a leader apart from other executives more clearly than a belief in and the use of a powerful and effective vision of the future.

Recent research by management scholars reveals several interesting characteristics about organizational visions. First, vision statements typically project 6 months to 20 years into the future (Kotter, 1990). Second, visions tend to be more "visionary" in organizations that are undergoing above-average industry or organizational change and for leaders who have a high level of discretion or control within their firm (Larwood, Falbe, Kriger, & Miesing, 1995). Third, vision effectiveness does *not* vary systematically by organization size, profit orientation, or leader demographics (Larwood et al., 1995).

Management research has also begun to show that effective organizational visions make a difference. For example, Oswald, Stanwick, and LaTour (1997) found that the more clear and inspiring the strategic vision was to the organization, the better the organizational performance. Collins and Porras (1994) discovered that the repeated succession of talented executives who care about the organizational vision is one of the key features that distinguishes extraordinary companies that pass the test of time from those firms that do not endure. And Oswald, Mossholder, and Harris (1994) found that the more salient the vision articulated by top management to the rest of the organization, the more effectively it functioned.

Despite its repeated emphasis, however, effective organizational visions are often viewed as a rare phenomenon. For example, Coulson-Thomas (1992) documented three different studies that confirm the importance of vision but disclose the disconnectedness between rhetoric and reality. In a national survey of executive leaders of the 1,000 largest firms, Truskie (1990) found that the ability to "create and inspire a shared vision" was the primary leadership behavior in which CEOs and presidents most often failed. And Bennis (1990) despairs that too many people in leadership positions focus on politics while ignoring their responsibility to create a vision of the future. In sum, the "vision thing," as George Bush called it (Stuart, 1994), is an ability to which many leaders aspire, but few achieve.

What Is Organizational Vision?

Ironically, organizational vision is supposed to provide clarity to those who follow it; but the term itself has many usages and a wide variety of understandings, so its meaning is not very clear. To quote Collins and Porras (1996), "Vision has become one of the most overused and least understood words in the language, conjuring up different images for different people: of deeply held values, outstanding achievement, societal bonds, exhilarating goals, motivating forces, or raisons d'être" (p. 66). An organizational vision is an image or metaphor or turn of words that fires up the imagination of the organization's employees. In fact, a successful vision requires "disciplined imagination" on the part of its creators if it is to capture the imagination of the rest of the organization (Shoemaker, 1997). In the muddled chaos of today's hyperturbulent environments, this vision provides a "north star" or "compass" to orient members of an organization to work together. Visions can be evolutionary or revolutionary (Beach, 1993), but they always require some "stretch" on the part of the organization to reach them (Hamel & Prahalad, 1989). An organizational vision creates something like a magnetic field that stimulates and directs energy within an organization (Wheatley, 1994).

Organizational visions are often codified into vision statements for the corporation. One of the most famous and dramatic vision statements was developed by Microsoft Corporation. From its beginning in 1975 until 1993, the company's vision statement was: "A computer on every desk and in every home." During this 18-year period, this vision served the company well (Abrahams, 1995). However, with the advent of the Internet, Microsoft must revise its thinking in terms of networks rather than individual computers. Thus, vision statements must be stable enough to provide direction but must also evolve over time. In sum, effective visions do two things. They provide a stable and unifying target or image for organizational members, and they motivate organizational members to reach for a new order.

Despite the legal necessity of attending to shareholders, "maximizing shareholder wealth does not inspire people at all levels of an organization, and it provides precious little guidance" (Collins & Porras, 1996, p. 66). Furthermore, Hamel and Prahalad (1989) argue that visions that do not identify unique and exemplary futures for the organization will not be effective. Consequently, organizational visions are unique creations of leaders, and they are never generic.

Just as the vision must be unique, visionary leaders are also distinctive. Westley and Mintzberg (1989) identify five different types of visionary leaders: creator, proselytizer, idealist, bricoleur,[1] and diviner; but they admit that there may be others as well. These authors liken visionary leadership to an interactive drama where an idea is created through practice and repetition. This idea is then represented to others as a vision, and then the "audience" assists in the amplification of the idea/vision through emotion and action. Thus, a visionary leader is like an artist attempting to evoke deeper stirrings within the followers.

Gary Hamel (1998), chairman of an innovative strategic consulting firm and visiting professor at the London Business School, emphasizes that the organizational vision must be innovative—not just for the organization but for the entire industry. He points out that academics, consultants, and planners for too long have ignored the creative process of strategic visioning while overemphasizing the analysis of existing visions and strategic actions inside and outside of the firm. In the new competitive environment, he argues that the ability to create a compelling and innovative new vision of the future that generates value for the customer will determine which organizations survive. Thus, vision is important and is becoming more important to organizational success and survival.

CEOs' Visions

In our general survey, I asked the respondents to state their vision of the future using the same open-ended question as Larwood et al.

(1995). Of the 91 respondents, more than three fourths (72) described their specific vision statements of the future. To determine the breadth and depth of these statements, I performed a content analysis of these statements. The results of this analysis are listed in Exhibit 6.1.

The most popular concepts are listed in italic type. As can be seen, the most common concept is the notion of being the "best" or "superior" or "excellent" (15 mentions). Interestingly, the second most common concept included in their vision statements focused on "customers" (14 mentions). The next four concepts all tied in popularity, and they focused on "community," "employees," "growth," and "quality" (10 mentions).

Although this information about frequency of concepts is interesting, it does not imply that the best vision includes all, or even any, of these ideas. Recall that the central purpose of a vision is to give direction and inspire members of an organization to stretch themselves. With this in mind, it is useful to see statements that illustrate each of these dimensions.

Guiding Visions

The fundamental purpose of a vision is to provide guidance and common direction to the members of the organization. A common direction is imperative in this age of self-interested behavior and turbulent environments. Below, I have listed several vision statements that fail to provide guidance or direction.

One CEO identified his firm's vision statement as follows: "a growing, compassionate enterprise of opportunity for those with whom the company is associated." Another CEO declared his vision statement as: "Have good chemistry and teamwork." A third CEO stated that his company vision is "to be a leader in our field." These statements may (or may not) be meaningful to the members of the organization, but they fail to provide much direction or guidance. They tend to be too process oriented to serve as a compass to the future. They lack specifics and content that guides (Larwood et al., 1995).

In contrast, the following statements are specific enough to focus energy within the organization. For example, one CEO identified his company's vision as "to emerge as a central force in the reformed health care system." As most observers note, the health care industry is under-

Exhibit 6.1 Content Analysis of CEOs' Vision Statements

Key Words/Concepts	Frequency
Accountable	1
Better the lives	1
Best/Exceeds expectations/Excellent/Premier/Superior/Top-tier/ Preferred	15
Central force	1
Community(s)/Community oriented	10
Compassionate	1
Competitors	1
Constituents	1
Consumers/Customers/Customer service/Guests	14
Disciplined	1
Do the right thing	1
Efficient	1
Employees/Human potential	10
Ethical	1
Exciting environments	1
Fair	1
Fulfillment/Fulfill responsibility	3
Fun/Have fun	4
Growth/Grow	10
Helpful	1
Honesty	1
Innovation	2
Integrity	2
Largest	1
Leadership/Leaders/Market leader	5
Nonfinancial and financial rewards	1
People helping people	1
Professionalism	1
Profit/Above-average profit/Make money	5
Quality/Quality products/High quality	10
Region	1
Respected/Recognized	4
Satisfaction	1
Selective segments	1
Shareholders/Owners/Stockholder value	6
Societal benefits	1
Team/Teamwork	5
Technology/High tech	3
World/International	3
Worth	1

NOTE: Concepts in italics were the most frequent or popular.

going tremendous changes currently. Some firms and professionals are leaving this industry, while new entrants are arriving almost daily. Competition is intense as the financing and delivery of care changes. This statement informs others that the leaders are confident about the future and are focused on understanding the changes occurring and positioning the firm to be "a central force" in the new marketplace.

Another CEO, whose company is in the transportation sector, identified his vision as follows: "to transition from a truck stop company to a travel center company over the next 3 years." This statement challenges the previous corporate identity, expands the identity of the organization to be a "travel center," and specifies a time frame for making the changes. Finally, in the banking industry, one CEO listed his vision as follows: "to become the bank of choice for the majority of professionals and small businesses in our market." This vision keeps the focus on particular segments in the banking industry.

If vision statements are to provide guidance, they must identify what the organization is not to become as well as what it is to become. Statements that lack direction focus too much on process without establishing certain boundary conditions. Visions that guide identify the content and nature of the future in a way that focuses work within the organization.

Inspiring Visions

Giving guidance means little unless the organizational members are also inspired to reach for the new order described in the vision. To inspire others requires some knowledge and understanding of matters that are bigger and more lasting than our limited day-to-day concerns. Of course, what brings inspiration to some people does not inspire others, and each vision is highly context dependent. Nonetheless, some vision statements ignore the human spirit, regardless of the context.

A CEO in the banking industry identified the following vision statement for his firm: "to achieve successful, positive growth in assets and income." It is hard to imagine bank tellers giving extraordinary and creative effort to see this vision realized. Similarly, in another bank, the vision identified was quite simply: "growth and profitability." Financially oriented vision statements are not limited to banking. A CEO of a manufacturing firm declared his firm's vision was "to grow and make money." Clearly, these vision statements are functionally oriented, but they fail to appeal to higher sensibilities in human beings.

Other vision statements are too vague to be inspiring. For example, the vision statement for a diversified firm was as follows: "to fulfill our responsibility to our constituents." Similarly, a telecommunications CEO listed the following vision statement: "to be a solid service provider." Finally, one CEO simply declared their organizational vision as "to work hard." The statements above are unimaginative and rather generic. They do not appeal to higher ideals within individuals. There is little energy behind the statements, and they are easily forgotten.

In contrast, some vision statements capture the imagination and stir the soul. A CEO in the hospitality industry seemed to understand this. He identified his vision as follows: "to offer exciting environments and to be legendary at creating smiles, laughter, and lasting memories with every guest we entertain." This statement makes one pause and take note. It catches your attention and energizes—it is inspiring.

A CEO in the energy business offered the following vision for his firm's future: "Steward resources and nurture relationships to help meet the world's need for safe, clean, reliable electricity." It is unusual to see the words *steward* and *nurture* in a company's guiding vision. These words stick with you. Furthermore, the vision concisely indicates that safety, environmental concerns, and reliability are guiding lights within the firm. These issues matter to most people in fundamental ways.

Also, a CEO in a high-technology firm indicated that his vision was "maximum development of *all* human potential within our company's influence—especially customers, employees, and shareholders." Here is a firm that was founded on technology, but its focus is human development—high tech balanced with high touch—an inspiring combination.

Another CEO used the "genius of the And" (Collins & Porras, 1994) by listing his desire for economic development and human development. His vision was "to cause the company to grow economically while providing a stimulating, rewarding, and fun experience for all our people." Notably, this CEO sees having fun and making money as reinforcing concepts, a unique combination and one that can inspire others.

Finally, a CEO in the construction industry identified his vision as follows: "We are a group of people who design, manufacture, sell, and service equipment to build and rebuild the world's infrastructure—

leaving our world better for the next generation." This conclusion of the statement uplifts workers: It suggests that longer term issues are of concern. There is a deep and universal human need to care for our off-spring and future generations. This vision statement taps into that need.

A listing of all vision statements provided by responding CEOs is provided in Exhibit 6.2. These statements are provided as examples of current vision statements in use, not necessarily as best practices. However, some of them are quite good and show careful thought and creativity.

Case Studies of CEOs' Visions

To round out our study of vision statements, we also examine the specific visions of the CEOs in our field study. Two of the CEOs, Robert Masters and Raymond Zuckerman, did not explicitly identify their vision for the organization. As a result, this section focuses on the five CEOs who did identify and are working toward a common vision for their respective organization.

Randy Maxwell

Recall that Randy was a big believer in envisioning positive outcomes and then preparing thoroughly to make that a reality. He was first introduced to the visioning process when serving as a helicopter pilot in Vietnam. On a daily basis, he envisioned his safe return to the United States despite the fact that bullets and rockets whizzed past him on each sortie.

Randy is a follower of the popular adage, "Do what you love and the money will follow" (Sinetar, 1987). But that raises the question, what is it that an organization can love? According to Randy, he wanted to create an organization that loves innovative technology that serves its three primary constituencies: customers, employees, and the share-holders. Consequently, the vision that Randy created for his firm was: "innovative technology for superior customer value, unparalleled opportunity of employee contribution and growth, and attractive shareholder return."

To make this vision widely shared, Randy had this statement framed and hung in numerous prominent places throughout the organization.

Exhibit 6.2 A Complete Listing of CEOs' Vision Statements

1. A caring organization that provides quality service and quality employment
2. Steward resources and nurture relationships to help meet the world's need for safe, clean, reliable electricity
3. To be the premier financial service organization in our community
4. Leadership
5. We are a group of people who design, manufacture, sell, and service equipment to build and rebuild the world's infrastructure—leaving our world better for the next generation
6. To be the best quick-service chain in the region
7. To work hard
8. To be a rapidly growing international technology company
9. A team that successfully builds a profitable company by facilitating the transformation of the local access communication networks and brings the power of information to consumers
10. To be the ethical, respected leader in our field
11. To cause the company to grow economically while providing a stimulating, rewarding, and fun experience for all our people
12. The future is acceptable as long as we identify the opportunities and plan positive results
13. Generate an opportunity to provide good products and opportunities for growth and fulfillment
14. To attain top-tier status in providing services to pharmaceutical and biotechnology companies
15. A leader in our field
16. To provide the highest quality corrections service in the world
17. To be recognized by our customers for providing the best service available within the tight lanes that we operate in
18. To be the best provider of investment banking services honestly and with integrity
19. To provide a quality of products and service which exceeds the expectations of our customers and which fairly rewards our owners and employees
20. To be the best in our industry
21. Maximum development of *all* human potential within our company's influence—especially customers, employees, shareholders
22. To be the world's preferred chemical company by customers, employees, investors, and suppliers
23. Innovative technology for superior customer value, unparalleled opportunity for employee contribution and growth, and attractive shareholder return
24. We perform our services with a covenant for quality; we treat our customers, shareholders, and each other fairly
25. A company that the customer thinks of first when there is a need
26. To be the best for all of our stakeholders and to excel in all endeavors
27. Maximization of return to community-based stockholder group while providing competent customer service
28. Continue to provide high quality financial products and services which satisfy the needs of our customers and community, ensure long-term profitability for our shareholders, and create opportunities for our employees
29. To meet our mission statement on a daily basis
30. To provide a service to our customers so our company will be their company of choice
31. To create a highly profitable and well-respected financial institution
32. Stay focused on people (employees & customers) and their needs and you will be successful
33. Have good chemistry and teamwork

(continued)

34. Growth for shareholders, opportunity for employees, contribution through product to better lives
35. To be the leading supplier of products to the high tech precision cleaning market
36. Disciplined growth in a cyclical business while maintaining above-average profitability
37. Growth and make money
38. Steady and consistent growth in profit and rewarding environment for employees
39. We will become a major supplier of networking equipment to improve our customers' bottom line
40. I would like our company to be both financially and operationally successful, resulting in broad respect by both our customers and competitors
41. To achieve growth and prosperity through helping our customers prosper and grow
42. Be progressive, innovative, and, without exception, committed to its employees, customers, and seek to broaden our network financially and geographically
43. To emerge as a central force in the reformed health care system
44. To be the best community banking organization in America—by any measure
45. Growth through disciplined practical experience
46. A growing, compassionate enterprise of opportunity for those with whom the company is associated
47. To be the premier hotel company in the world by providing high quality, value-based lodging brands in selective segments
48. To provide leadership which is rewarding to our employees, customers, and owners (shareholders); *rewarding* is defined more broadly than financial rewards
49. Teamwork will assure continued growth
50. Quality without compromise
51. Respected and considered successful by competitors, shareholders, employees, and the community
52. To be the premier company in our industry
53. To be a solid service provider
54. Achieve value for shareholders and benefits for society
55. Working as a team will allow us to grow and maintain our market leadership position
56. Growth, quality products, and service
57. To achieve successful, positive growth in assets and income
58. To be the best community oriented financial services company in Virginia
59. To create a successful enterprise, overcoming a problem past
60. Be acknowledged as the leader in customer service in our field
61. Growth and profitability
62. Dedicated to our motto "People Helping People" Independent—very community-minded
63. Organization that strives to increase shareholder value through people and that provides sense of satisfaction and sense of worth to all its employees
64. One that is fair and helpful to its customers and the communities it serves
65. To fulfill our responsibility to our constituents
66. A community-oriented organization
67. Our organization should make money, have fun, and always do the right thing for the employees, customers, and shareholders
68. To be a provider of high-quality news and information in the markets we serve
69. To transition from a truck stop company to a travel center company over the next 3 years
70. To offer exciting environments and to be legendary at creating smiles, laughter, and lasting memories with every guest we entertain
71. Recognized as an organization that is responsible to its customers, employees, and shareholders needs
72. To become the bank of choice for the majority of professionals and small businesses in our market

At each planning session, the vision statement was revisited by his top management team; the focus was first put on enhancing customer value through innovation. Also, annual performance evaluations for each employee began with examinations of how the person contributed to the firm's vision statement. And in day-to-day conversations, Randy attempted to inject this vision into employee's thinking. As demonstrated by all this activity, this vision was central to Randy's activities.

Michael Breen

Before Michael told me his vision, he stated,

> We are starting to create something special here. The whole change in this company and the proposed direction is becoming very, very contagious. And it is really starting to show up in a lot of things that we're doing. It's showing up, certainly, in our financials. Even more important, it is showing in people's attitudes.

Quite simply, the vision statement of his corporation is: "to be the best community bank in the nation—by any measure." According to Michael, increasing numbers of employees were starting to think: "Wow, being the best is really a possibility!" The power of identifying what is possible was changing attitudes, and this led to changed behaviors, according to the CEO.

Interestingly, the bank had already become one of the best banks in the nation using typical industry measures. This worried Michael, as he did not want his employees to become complacent. He states, "I don't want people to think that we've ever made it, that we've arrived. There is always one more thing to be done, one more road we have not yet taken."

Michael disclosed that Jesus was the exemplar in creating and pursuing his vision statement. He was particularly guided by the following actions of Christ:

> Christ clearly challenged the status quo. He disturbed comfort zones in a major, major way. He clearly inspired people with his vision of what is possible, and he obviously recognized that he needed to empower his disciples. Finally, he reminded his

disciples: "Hey guys, I am not going to be around here for a long time so you need to be keepers of the vision too."

Michael concluded that his central role as CEO is "to be nurturing the vision of the future." Clearly, he places paramount importance on this aspect of his leadership role.

Richard Farr

The vision statement for Richard's bank was: "to create a highly profitable and well-respected financial institution." Richard saw the visioning process as part of his larger role as chief strategist within the firm. He found that the vision statement was helpful during strategy sessions with other members of the top management team. He recalls,

> We occasionally sit down and strategize and look at future crossroads. There are times in your firm's development when you need to stop and think about options for the future. We spend hours talking about these options and sometimes the vision statement pops up and helps us to eliminate options that don't fit with it.

So the vision statement is more like a tool in Richard's strategy tool kit. It does not appear to be widely distributed throughout the organization, but it does help clarify strategic options. In Richard's words, "It helps us do what is right."

Steven Zolte

Like Richard, Steven uses the vision statement to clarify the decision-making process. However, he encouraged its distribution throughout the organization more than Richard did, as Steven saw it as a useful communication mechanism to the entire organization. He stated, "I want our employees to know the priorities in this firm and the vision statement helps me to do just that." Steven emphasized forceful execution of a simple but logical strategy over the creation of a brilliant but complex strategy. To make things clear and simple, he created the following vision statement for his firm: "disciplined growth in a cyclical business while maintaining above-average profitability."

Steven acknowledged that this statement was not inspiring nor was it particularly creative, but that did not bother him. In his mind, the key issue is "to keep it simple." He reasoned,

> Everyone in our organization knows what we are doing. With all the hype about empowerment, I think you empower people by giving them information and direction. If it is consistent, they can go and execute because they know what they're supposed to be doing. And they don't waste their time worrying about whether or not it is in line. Then all the energy goes into making the firm competitive rather than becoming embroiled in organizational politics.

In sum, Steven saw vision statements as a means for clarifying direction so that employees would be empowered to act in concert with each other. He did not see it as an inspirational tool; rather, it was a mechanism for simplifying work and focusing energy.

Joseph Henderson

Joseph saw himself as a diviner of changes in a rapidly changing health care market. As a result, his guiding vision was: "to emerge as a central force in the reformed health care system."

Joseph argued that all this change in health care was creating havoc in health care organizations. He noticed that the uncertain future of the health care marketplace not only caused some leading firms to falter but also created opportunities for those with entrepreneurial instincts to provide greater value to customers. Consequently, his vision statement acknowledged that things were changing dramatically, but it also encouraged its listeners to believe in the future of the firm. In this way, it instilled hope, which is a precious commodity in a turbulent industry.

Summing Up

Creative new visions of the future are essential for success in our new, information-based economy. Although all agree that effective visions are a hallmark of leadership, few leaders take the time or know how to tap their creative juices to produce them. In a content analysis of the CEOs' vision statements, the most common ideas expressed in vision statements concern notions of excellence, quality, customer value, and community well-being. However, the most effective vision statements are unique to the people and circumstances, so the most common concepts are not necessarily the most effective.

All of the CEO vision statements were listed to give the readers ideas and examples of the content of specific visions. In the analysis of these statements, I attempted to identify exemplars among this set of vision statements according to two criteria: amount of guidance provided and its inspirational quality. As this is a creative endeavor, a vision statement is more a work of art than a leadership technique.

Collective Shadow Work With Vision

Just as the leader must engage his own shadow, he must also be prepared to discern and work with the collective shadow within the organization. Because vision is an organizational-level phenomenon, the absence of organizational vision suggests that it is buried somewhere in the collective shadow of the organization's culture. This section offers some ideas for identifying and exploring how the vision is hidden within the collective shadows of the organization.

1. Vision statements are popular and ubiquitous in organizations today; however, very few employees know or care about these vision statements. Why do you think that this is so?

2. One popular method for identifying individual visions of the future involves writing out your own eulogy as you would like it to be (Covey, 1989). The same approach can be taken by writing the eulogy of your organization. Do this with other members of your organization and compare and contrast these eulogies. What did you learn from this experience?

3. *Dilbert* cartoons characterize the collective shadow that pervades many organizations today. *Dilbert* is an enormously popular cartoon series featured in 700 newspapers and in six books written by

Scott Adams. These cartoons satirize organizations by poking fun at those in leadership roles, and they celebrate the lack of creativity and unproductive uses of time that workers experience. Although there is a sad accuracy to this general depiction, Scott Adams does not offer a way out of this situation.[2] In the absence of vision, there is organizational cynicism. How pervasive is the dark and shadowy expression of cynicism in your workplace? What would a leader have to do to break through this organizational cynicism? Are you that leader?

Notes

1. The term *bricoleur* refers to a common figure in France: a man who frequents junkyards and picks up stray bits and pieces and combines them to make new objects. In this context, Westley and Mintzberg (1989) used this term to denote the visionary's ability to create a new gestalt after reviewing the various objects within and without the organization.

2. I owe this idea to a personal conversation with Lee Bolman, who is currently working on a management book that reflects on the *Dilbert* phenomenon.

7

Creating Effective Strategic Priorities

Visionary companies pursue a cluster of objectives of which making money is only one and not necessarily the primary one.
— James Collins & Jerry Porras, 1994, p. 55

The test of a first-rate intelligence is the ability to hold two opposing ideas in mind at the same time and still retain the ability to function.
— F. Scott Fitzgerald, 1956, p. 69

Present management thinking about a healthy organization may be oversimplified and at times false.
— Chris Argyris, 1958, p. 107

The second creative fruit of executive leadership is the establishment of clear strategic priorities within the firm. The first creative fruit of leadership (i.e., a vision of the future) gives the organization its general direction and provides a source of inspiration. The strategic priorities provide more tangible milestones that help to realize the vision. Effective leaders who have engaged with their shadows know how to develop vision and establish priorities to focus energy expended within the organization. For those in leadership positions who have failed to engage their shadow, their personal and organizational priorities are unclear and energy is scattered.

Clear and widely shared priorities give the organization its focus by specifying the intermediate outcomes that are most desired. Clear priorities bring a cohesiveness to organizational life. Previous research has shown that innovation is accelerated and enhanced when the leaders clearly specify the outcomes desired but leave the means for achieving those outcomes unspecified (Judge, Fryxell, & Dooley, 1997).

When strategic priorities are unclear in an organization, there is a lack of focus, and self-interested behavior often becomes the norm. In the absence of clear priorities from executive leaders, employees are left to speculate as to what the priorities are. This often leads to fragmentation on the part of the organization and suboptimal behavior (Richards, 1986), especially in times of crisis (Quinn, 1980). When leaders are more concerned with their leadership position than with the organization they lead, this approach is most common.

Having clear strategic priorities does not mean that there is only *one* priority, however. In a recent survey of 132 chief financial officers of various public and private companies, 66% of the respondents indicated that they attempt to pursue multiple strategic priorities and provide value to more than one stakeholder group (Birchard, 1995). Even financial economists acknowledge the growing relevance of multiple strategic priorities by recognizing implicit and explicit claims against corporate assets (Cornell & Shapiro, 1987).

Recent research by Collins and Porras (1994) has shown that providing value to multiple stakeholder groups is the key to enduring excellence. To use their memorable phrase, "Visionary companies avoid the 'Tyranny of the OR' and liberate themselves to the 'Genius of the AND'" (p. 44). In short, multiple strategic priorities, both financial and nonfinancial in their focus, must be emphasized by executive leaders if their companies are to survive and indeed prosper.

Perhaps this is why the "balanced scorecard" approach to tracking and guiding strategic efforts is so popular currently. The balanced scorecard was developed by Robert Kaplan and David Norton (1992), and its aim is to provide a set of measures that track progress against the firm's strategic priorities in a holistic and timely fashion. This approach has challenged executives to consider a broad array of financial and operational measures rather than focusing on one financial measure exclusively. The clarity achieved and complexity covered by such an approach allows executives to pursue multiple strategic priorities at the same time. Furthermore, it can help executives link future strategic priorities to current strategic actions (Kaplan & Norton, 1996).

Prioritization Schemas

One of the most common ways to establish priorities is to create a hierarchy where "basic" priorities must be met before addressing "high-level" priorities. For example, Abraham Maslow (1954) observed that individuals have a hierarchy of needs ranging from our most basic physical needs (e.g., physiological and safety) to social needs (e.g., affiliation with others and esteem from others) to our highest set of needs (e.g., self-actualization of personal values). Organizations have also been observed to have a needs hierarchy. Tuzzolino and Armandi (1981) identified the needs of organizations to range from its most basic needs (e.g., profitability and cash flow), to social needs (e.g., belonging to a community of organizations and having a positive reputation), to its highest set of needs (e.g., serving multiple internal and external stakeholder groups).

Although these hierarchical ordering approaches are relatively clear and straightforward, some people argue that this approach is not realistic in practice due to the interdependent nature of an organization's constituencies (Freeman & Gilbert, 1988; Singer, 1994). Their alternative is to identify multiple priorities, note their interdependencies, but refuse to order one as most important or more basic than another one. This nonhierarchical or "networked" approach is more complex to explain to others and is not as straightforward to implement as the hierarchical approach, but it acknowledges the interrelated nature of priorities and treats them as a holistic system.

Exhibit 7.1 offers a graphical depiction of the two prioritization schemes discussed above. By way of example, I illustrate two ways to prioritize various aspects of human life, using each of the two approaches. One common way to conceptualize a human life is its three dimensions: body, mind, and spirit. If a person was asked to "order" these three dimensions, a common approach might be to arrange them in a hierarchy of tangibility where the body is placed at the base, the mind in the middle, and the spirit is placed at the apex of the hierarchy. Alternatively, a networked ordering would be to place all three aspects

Exhibit 7.1 Hierarchical Versus Networked Prioritization Schemes

---

I. Hierarchical Ordering of Relationship Between Body, Mind, and Spirit

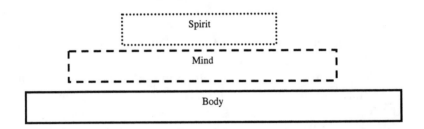

II. Networked Ordering of Relationship Between Body, Mind, and Spirit

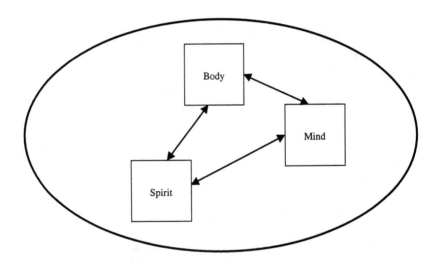

on the same level, arguing that they are interrelated to such a degree that to place them in some sort of hierarchy would distort their interdependent nature. The point here is not to argue for one approach over the other but to be aware of different ordering principles. This has relevance to our later examination of ordering strategic priorities.

Priorities Assigned to Stakeholder Groups

The first set of strategic priorities addressed in this chapter concerns the identification and relative weighting of the most important organizational stakeholders. An organizational stakeholder is a group of people who hold some strong interest or "stake" in the organization's future performance (Freeman, 1984). Clearly, there is a wide variety of stakeholders for every organization, but the four most common groups are: (a) owners or shareholders, (b) customers or consumers, (c) employees or contractors, and (d) the local community. Previous research has shown that the best organizations must serve multiple stakeholder groups well (Collins & Porras, 1994; Donaldson & Preston, 1995; Kotter & Heskett, 1992). Leaders must clarify in words and deed what the relative importance is for its primary stakeholder groups.

There are several notable examples of stakeholder prioritization by executive leaders. The earliest direct statement of stakeholder prioritization was established by James Lincoln, former CEO of the Lincoln Electric Company (Sharplin, 1994). At the turn of the century, Mr. Lincoln identified the top three stakeholder groups, and he listed them (hierarchically) as: (a) customers, (b) employees, and (c) stockholders. This prioritization has continued throughout the century, and this clear set of priorities has created an enduring framework for a very successful business. More recently, Kotter and Heskett (1992) observed that such highly successful companies as Hewlett-Packard, Wal-Mart, and Dayton Hudson employ stakeholder perspectives.

Some executives and academics argue that giving priority to more than one stakeholder group is too impractical and idealistic (e.g., Kaplan & Norton, 1996). However, the esteemed former president and recently retired chairman of Canon, Ryuzaburo Kaku (1997), has passionately argued that executive leaders, particularly those leading global multinational corporations, need to learn to cooperate with a broad range of stakeholders groups if the world is to survive. He calls this approach *kyosei,* and he concludes,

If corporations run their businesses with the sole aim of gaining more market share or earning more profits, they may well lead the world into economic, environmental, and social ruin. But

Exhibit 7.2 CEOs' Prioritization of Four Primary Stakeholder Groups
($N = 89$)

Stakeholder Group	Lowest Weighting	Highest Weighting	Average Weighting	Median Weighting
Owners	0.0%	100.0%	30.0%	30.0%
Customers	0.0%	75.0%	33.7%	30.0%
Employees	0.0%	50.0%	25.3%	25.0%
Community	0.0%	25.0%	10.9%	10.0%

NOTE: Respondents were asked to distribute a total of 100 percentage points across the four stakeholder groups according to the priority that they placed on these groups.

if they work together, in a spirit of kyosei, they can bring food to the poor, peace to war-torn areas, and renewal to the natural world. (p. 63)

In essence, a highly successful multinational business leader is suggesting that one of the most *impractical* things executive leaders can do is pursue their narrow financial interests.

Other observers of business have come to the same conclusion as Kaku. For example, Orts (1992) noted a drift in corporate law to emphasize the stakeholder concept over the stockholder concept. Jones (1995) concluded that a trustworthy and cooperative approach to stakeholders is actually more efficient than an approach that is untrustworthy, uncooperative, or both. And Clarkson (1995) reports higher survival rates for firms pursuing the multiple stakeholder orientation over the traditional stockholder orientation.

Because stakeholders have different interests, conflicts among stakeholder demands are likely. The specter of multiple conflicting interests requires that executive leaders learn how to sort out tradeoffs between the varying stakeholder groups (Clarkson, 1995). Consequently, our survey of executives in leadership positions asked them to allocate 100 percentage points between the four primary stakeholder groups to reflect the relative importance of each group. Exhibit 7.2 reveals the results of that inquiry.

Exhibit 7.2 shows that, on average, the customers (33.7%) and the owners (30.0%) are the top stakeholder priorities for executive leaders. However, the employees (25.3%) are close behind in emphasis across all the executive leaders surveyed. Community concerns are often considered, but these are given the least attention among the four stakeholder groups, with an average allocation of 10.9%. Interestingly, there is a considerable range of priorities given to each stakeholder group across all respondents. For example, some executives awarded 100% of their attention to owners whereas others invested none of their attention to owners. The range of interest in customers was from 0% to 75%, and the range for employees was 0% to 50%. This variation in interest suggests that there is no widely accepted norm of stakeholder prioritization among executive leaders.

Priorities Assigned to Strategic Goals

The second set of priorities that needs to be established by executive leaders is the organization's strategic goals. Strategic goals translate stakeholder priorities into actionable events. Although there is debate as to how specific these strategic goals need to be (Quinn, 1980), there is agreement that strategic goals are useful for focusing organizational attention in a common direction (Richards, 1986).

Recent research has shown that there are three dimensions that can be used to identify strategic goals: (a) internal capabilities, (b) external conditions, and (c) time (Fiegenbaum, Hart, & Schendel, 1996). According to this perspective, executive leaders must select the strategic goals along one or more of these dimensions to establish a *strategic reference point* (SRP) for their firm. It is theorized that firms will be risk averse when the firm is operating above its SRP and risk takers when below (worse than) its SRP (Kahneman & Tversky, 1979).

Once strategic goals are selected, these goals constrain and guide the strategic decision-making process (Donaldson & Lorsch, 1983). Of course, strategic goals are often revised as the firm gets feedback on its progress against these goals; but it is not uncommon for this revision process to occur slowly over a period of years (Fiegenbaum et al., 1996). When the organization's future is uncertain due to crisis conditions, the number of strategic goals often is reduced, and goals are made much more specific than during noncrisis situations (Quinn, 1980).

Exhibit 7.3 documents the strategic goals emphasized by the executive leaders in the research study. Each CEO was presented with a listing of 12 common strategic goals and asked to indicate the level of

Exhibit 7.3 CEOs' Prioritization of 12 Strategic Goals ($N = 90$)

Strategic Goal	Not Important at All (%)	Moderately Important (%)	Extremely Important (%)
Net profit	0.0	5.5	94.5
Rate of growth	3.3	34.4	62.1
Market share	13.3	36.7	49.9
Employee morale	1.1	5.6	93.2
Customer satisfaction	0.0	1.1	98.9
Company prestige	8.0	36.4	55.6
Innovation	5.5	25.6	68.8
Assets and reserves	8.8	35.6	55.5
Dividend payout	60.6	19.1	20.2
Quality/price leadership	3.3	18.9	77.8
Service to community	12.1	30.0	57.7
Equipment/plant modernness	20.1	40.0	43.7

importance of each goal. Their potential responses ranged from a 1 or 2 (*not important at all*) to a 3 (*moderately important*) to a 4 or 5 (*extremely important*). The CEOs indicated that the following goals were most often viewed to be extremely important: (a) customer satisfaction (98.9%), (b) net profit (94.5%), and (c) employee morale (93.2%). Interestingly, the strategic goals of little or no importance to the CEOs were (a) dividend payout (60.6%), (b) equipment/plant modernness (20.1%), and (c) market share (13.3%).

It is important to note that the strategic goals correspond to the stakeholder priorities discussed earlier. One would expect that the emphasis of customers and owners and employee stakeholder groups would be reflected in strategic goals directed at these three groups. Indeed, this was the case as customer satisfaction reflects the customers' interests, net profit reflects the owners' interests, and employee morale reflects the employees' interests. Notably, the relative importance of stakeholder groups (i.e., customers > owners > employees) corresponds to the relative importance of strategic goals (i.e., customer satisfaction > net profit > employee morale). In sum, there appears to be consistency between the stakeholder priorities and goal priorities set by executive leaders. In addition, multiple priorities are the norm, not the exception, for the respondents in this study.

Case Studies of CEOs' Priorities

Robert Masters

Robert stressed that it was the responsibility of his top management team, not just himself, to decide the firm's strategic priorities. However, he was intimately involved in establishing and revising the strategic priorities and viewed himself as most responsible for this process. His team consisted of his chief financial officer, his vice president of manufacturing, and himself. Here is how the prioritization process unfolds at his firm:

> The three of us sit down and talk about what are realistic goals and priorities. These talks range from what kind of gross margin can you make and still be competitive all the way to philosophical issues of what is important and right. We do this on a regular and an ad hoc basis. It is an ongoing dialogue. It seems to work pretty well as we all have different viewpoints, but there is listening going on, too.

At the time that this study was conducted, the process described above yielded an equal emphasis on the owners, customers, and employee stakeholder groups (30% each), with the remainder on the local community in which his operation existed (10%). Their current strategic goals were primarily focused on four areas: net profit, employee morale, customer satisfaction, and quality leadership in the environmental incineration industry. Because of the firm's recent emergence from bankruptcy, company prestige was also emphasized: Its reputation had been tarnished in previous years. However, Robert anticipated that this emphasis would fade over time as their troubled past faded in customers' and suppliers' memories.

Michael Breen

Michael had an interesting and rather unconventional approach to pursuing his strategic priorities. He said,

> You can take two approaches to strategic priorities in a publicly held firm. You can say, "Boy, I've got to make the numbers, I've got to make the numbers, I've got to make the numbers." Or you can say, "I can do all the right things and the numbers will take care of themselves." I sort of believe in the second approach.

However, he does not ignore progress against numerical goals. He stated,

> Now, a lot of people need to have numbers out there; they need to see the numbers; they need to see the goals. I don't necessarily need to have those embedded in my brain—my CFO does. He loves that kind of stuff.

Commenting on how the strategic priorities are established in his firm, he went on to say,

> You know, certainly, I have a strong team around me, and we jointly develop our priorities. They are actively involved in our long-term financial and strategic goals. At the same time, I sort of put my own stretch targets out there. And you know, as a publicly held company, we listen to Wall Street pretty closely, although we try to prevent what I believe is a short-term mentality that comes along with listening to Wall Street. You have got to live quarter by quarter, but I try to keep it more long-term focused than quarter-by-quarter focused. You see others are constantly trying to compartmentalize our firm and my life into narrow categories, and I won't permit that. By fighting this compartmentalization, I can live more consistently. I try to impress that on our team, and it seems to be getting through to them.

This prioritization process yielded an equal weighting of owner, customer, and employee stakeholder groups (30% each), with the remaining 10% weighting to the local communities in which Michael's banks operated. However, in keeping with his vision of being the best community banking company—by any measure—Michael listed almost all of the strategic goals as extremely important. Indeed, of the 12 strategic goals listed, only 2 goals (i.e., equipment/plant modernness and company prestige) were listed as moderately important. Therefore, Michael's vision guided his strategic priorities; whereas his priorities were quite broad and comprehensive, his personal focus was narrowly focused on his vision. Paradoxically, Michael both emphasized and ignored "the numbers" in his pursuit of the future.

Joseph Henderson

Joseph liked to "set the stage" each year for his employees by describing key industry trends and discussing the resultant priorities within the firm for the future. This allowed him to lay out his assumptions for the entire organization to see and act accordingly. He was very concerned that people inside and outside of the organization understand the logic being used by him and his top management team. Here is a description of his recent "stage setting" to the employees:

> I try to tell the troops how we view the world each year. Recently, I told them that health care reform is well under way and that it is market driven, it is not government driven. As a result, managed care is the key to the future; and this places a much greater focus on reducing the cost of health care. However, the quality of health care will be an evolving issue as we deliver less care over time. Because of this reform, competitive alignments and networks are forming at a rapid pace. The fact is that it is physicians that drive the value in these networks. So creating win/win relationships with physicians is key to our future.

Joseph said that stakeholder priorities are relatively fixed over time. Notably, he rated each of the four stakeholder groups equally, with a 25% relative rating. In contrast, the company's strategic goals shift from year to year. He initially develops those strategic goals by himself and then offers them to his top management team. The team then challenges those goals, and they then revise the goals together. Eventually, they end up with "something that we can agree on," and a letter from the president is mailed to each and every employee. Interestingly, Joseph listed all strategic goals as extremely important except for dividend payout and equipment/plant modernness.

Richard Farr

Richard was part of a three-member executive committee composed of himself, the chairman, and chief operating officer. These three individuals determined the strategic priorities and direction for their bank holding company. They do not have regularly scheduled meetings to discuss priorities; their meetings tend to be more event driven. Here is Richard's account:

> We don't have scheduled meetings to discuss these issues. We just meet whenever it is important. We are together often on loan committee meetings. You know, banks are dominated by loan committee meetings, and we three are often together in these sessions. At the end or beginning of these meetings, we often discuss our priorities. However, sometimes we sit together to discuss these things in a dedicated fashion when new opportunities arise. There are times when your bank has several options in front of it, and you've got this option and that option to consider. Those are the times when we tend to spend hours and hours talking about the different options.

Richard commented that they did not run the bank the way academics say you should, but they were reluctant to change due to the bank's strong results. In his own words,

> Sometimes I worry that we aren't doing it the way the textbooks say to do it, that we aren't more structured, that we don't have a 5-year or 10-year plan. And I worry about how we can be successful as we've not been doing it the way you are supposed to do it. But then, we are very successful. It seems that the textbooks limit flexibility and the opportunity to be creative. Our unstructured approach has capitalized on that.

In sum, Richard took a rather unstructured, opportunistic approach to the prioritization process. Priorities tended to emerge over time as opportunities presented themselves. This approach allowed for a more entrepreneurial style of banking that Richard credited for the bank's success. However, he worried that the approach was too unstructured and not comprehensive enough, particularly as the bank grew.

The bank's current stakeholder priorities were primarily focused on customers and employees (30% each), but there was also a relatively high emphasis on the owners and local community (20% each). In keeping with its entrepreneurial approach, the bank's strategic goals were partially congruent with stakeholder priorities, which Richard identified as customer satisfaction (congruent with the customer emphasis) and net profit (inconsistent with reduced emphasis on owners or shareholders).

Raymond Zuckerman

Raymond's top management team was responsible for creating and revising the strategic priorities for the firm. In this case, the team was called the management committee, and it comprised the CEO, the chief financial officer (CFO), the president, the head merchant, the head of operations, and the human resources director. This committee takes a very structured approach to setting strategic priorities over a series of meetings.

First, they meet to examine how the firm performed against targets set the previous year; the CFO leads this discussion. Then, they jointly work to determine what their firm's goals and priorities need to be in the future. After that, they meet again to revise the target levels after thinking more about the goals, and they discuss strategies for reaching these goals. When this committee agrees to the goals and priorities, it is proposed to the board of directors, who also debate and discuss these ideas. Notably, the central focus is on financial goals, especially earnings projections, but other goals are discussed as constraining or facilitating the meeting of those goals.

Despite this strong focus on increasing shareholder value, Raymond emphasized customer (45% relative weighting) and employee (50% weighting) stakeholder groups over the owner groups (5% weighting). In his opinion, "If you take care of your customers and employees, everything falls into place later on." However, he noted that his firm had failed to meet performance goals for several years in the recent past, so there was a special urgency to improve shareholder value.

Perhaps this is why Raymond listed net profit as an extremely important strategic goal despite the relative lack of importance of owner satisfaction. In addition to profitability, he also emphasized employee morale, customer satisfaction, innovation, and quality/price leadership. Overall, there was little consistency between his stakeholder priorities and strategic goal priorities.

Randy Maxwell

Randy gets together with his five direct reports on a regular basis, and they systematically develop their strategic priorities. First, they revisit their vision of the future and check to make sure that it is still relevant. This is typically achieved by gathering his top management team at an off-site retreat. They then review their progress against the previous year's goals and priorities and begin to discuss the future. At the conclusion of the meeting, Randy summarizes their discussion in a document; then, he circulates that document among his team after the meeting. During this discussion, they can make comments and suggestions to change these targets and priorities; after several iterations, a fresh set of priorities is established and communicated to the rest of the organization. In Randy's own words,

> After meeting at an off-site location, I'll take their input and put some language around it. Then I circulate it around and solicit their comments. This usually takes several iterations and some word crafting is necessary. My direct reports and I will then go to the rest of the company and say, "Alright, this is where we are going to go." We lay it out for the entire company to see. If they have questions, we get them answers. Then the employees start to lay out their personal and departmental goals in an effort to support the overall organizational goals. It is a layered, iterative process.

According to Randy, his firm is primarily focused on customers (40% weighting), is secondarily focused on the employees and owners (25% each), and allocates 10% of its attention to community issues. These stakeholder priorities were translated into four key strategic goal domains: employee morale, customer satisfaction, innovation, and quality/price leadership. There do appear to be linkages between stakeholder emphasis and strategic goals at this firm.

Steven Zolte

Steven explained that the strategic prioritization process was driven by external realities. In essence, he argued that you begin by knowing your industry context (as this book recommends). He stated,

> You set your priorities based on business fundamentals—in our case, we have a very specific strategy of growing our business that participates in a consolidating industry. This simple fact drives all that we do here—long-term thinking and execution are essential. There is little room for miscalculation or incomplete thinking.

Given this context, Steven and his top management team gather regularly to discuss new goals and/or progress against previous goals. If there is disagreement on the specific goals or goal conflicts, Steve decides. According to him, "I always strive for consensus; but if we can't achieve it, then it is my call."

Steven explained that there is considerable illegal and unethical behavior going on in his markets. He observed that some of his competitors engage in these behaviors to gain short-term competitive advantages. However, he believes that it is not in the interest of his company or the industry to participate in such activities. He stated,

> There are a lot of things that you can do in our industry that are inappropriate. And there are companies out there that do that. For example, there are companies that make payoffs to politicians. Now I can assure you that in my 15 years with this company, we have operated in a clean, "no short-cuts" fashion. In the long run, we will succeed, and our competitors who cut corners will fail due to lack of integrity.

According to Steven, his firm values owners, customers, and employees equally (30% weighting each), with residual attention going to the local community (10%). Currently, his strategic goals are aimed at hitting targets related to net profit, market share, sales growth, and customer satisfaction. Reflecting on their past and future, Steven proudly noted,

> In the last 5 years, we've grown 22% per year. Now, I'm 52—I'll retire 10 years from now at 62. If we hit our earnings targets of 15% after-tax return on equity and 18% growth in sales over that period, then we will grow from being a $722 million company to a $3 billion company when I retire. It is going to be fun and interesting to see if we can achieve what we have set out to do.

Summing Up

The organizational vision provides the future image that guides and motivates its members to move forward in a cooperative fashion. To further refine this movement, strategic priorities must be determined and communicated to the rest of the organization. In this chapter, we examined two priority systems that must be established by executive leaders: stakeholder groups and strategic goals. In the past, the only stakeholder groups that mattered were the owners; the only strategic goals of interest were financial, especially net profit. Leaders today must cope with multiple stakeholder demands, and, hence, there must be multiple strategic goals pursued simultaneously. However, they must also avoid having too many priorities, which can defeat the purpose of having any priorities at all.

Based on survey responses, the most common ordering of stakeholder priority is: (a) customers, (b) owners, (c) employees, and (d) local community(s). Consistent with this stakeholder prioritization, the most popular strategic goals are: (a) customer satisfaction, (b) net profit, and (c) employee morale. Considering previous research and our data, it is clear that executive leaders must have clear priorities set and communicated to the rest of the organization.

From our field studies, we also learned several things. First, the creation and revision of strategic priorities is a regular and ongoing part of executive leadership positions. Second, the top management team is usually involved in this process as well. Third, the larger the organization, the more formal and structured this process is. Finally, there may or may not be consistency between the stated stakeholder priorities and the strategic goals pursued.

Collective Shadow Work
With Strategic Priorities

Just as organizational cynicism is evidence of the need for shadow work on organizational vision, fragmentation within the organization is evidence of the need for shadow work on strategic priorities. When an organization is fragmented, there is no alignment of priorities, so individual and departmental priorities operate independently of each other. When the collective shadow casts a darkness over the entire organization, the priorities are perceived by organizational members to be either too numerous to enable focused attention or too singular to develop a balanced approach.

When confronted with the "too many priorities" syndrome, organizations have not learned their unique collective "gift," nor have they acknowledged their special place in the world. In the company's attempt to "be all things to all people," the energy within the organization is not focused, fragmentation ensues, and the organization deteriorates. In extreme cases, the organization dies.

When confronted with the "too few priorities" syndrome, organizations have not learned they are interdependently linked with their environment. These organizations narrowly pursue service to a single stakeholder while neglecting other stakeholders; or they pursue a narrow set of goals while ignoring complementary goals that ensure long-term survival. In extreme cases, illegal activities take place as a result of this syndrome.

The only antidote to these syndromes is a more holistic focus on organizational health. Healthy organizations have a balanced set of strategic priorities. They know what their unique contribution is to society, and they understand that their organization is inextricably linked with the larger society. The organization continuously grows and develops its people, and its core competencies manifest themselves in creative and value-added ways. Notably, there is a vitality within healthy organizations and often a well-regarded reputation outside of the organization.

There is no one way to ensure individual health; the same applies to organizational health. However, the following activities may be useful in the assessment or treatment of organizational health problems:

Organizational Health Assessment:

- Identify the "culture gap" by surveying employees on the difference between the actual and ideal organizational culture (Kilmann & Saxton, 1991)
- Compare the organization's practices to the best practices in its primary industry
- Conduct a retreat to collectively reflect on the organization's health
- Hire a competent organizational development consultant to report on the organization's health
- Ask key external and internal stakeholders to collectively share their views on the organization's effectiveness

Organizational Health Interventions:

- Conduct a "future search" conference where 40 to 100 participants gather over a 2- to 3-day period in a search for common ground (Weisbord & Janoff, 1995)
- Conduct a "real time strategic change" where hundreds if not thousands of participants gather over a 2- to 3-day period in an effort to identify and accelerate systemwide changes (Jacobs, 1994)
- Initiate a "workout" where an organizational health problem is identified by an intact work group and where process improvements are identified over 1 to 2 days (Bunker & Alban, 1997)
- Using "open space technology," conduct periodic town meetings for sharing information across interest groups over 1 to 3 days (Owen, 1993)

In all these assessment or intervention activities, strive for clear strategic priorities but watch for collective shadows that prevent a clear and reasoned consensus of what those priorities are. Recognize that this is a continuous process and that prevention is more effective than cure.

Creating Organizational Trust

The changing psychological contract is driving the business world toward an individualistic workforce–men and women who place their trust not in corporations but in their own capabilities, self-entrepreneurs who run their careers like privately held corporations.

— Michael Marks, 1988, p. 39

Trust is mandatory for optimization of a system. Without trust, there cannot be cooperation between people, teams, departments, or divisions. Without trust, each component will protect its own immediate interests to its own long-term detriment, and to the detriment of the entire system. Transformation is required. Transformation begins with the individual. The job of the leader is to create an environment of trust so that everyone may confidently examine himself.

— W. Edward Deming, quoted in Whitney, 1993, p. viii

The third and final creative fruit of executive leaders is the development of trust between organizational members. Even if the vision is clear and inspiring (creative fruit No. 1) and the strategic priorities are brilliant and balanced (creative fruit No. 2), nothing happens without organizational trust. In this age of global competition, revolutionary new technologies, and shortened time horizons, uncertainty threatens to paralyze all but the fearless or the ignorant. Organizational trust is a major antidote to this new world order. Increasing numbers of leaders and observers argue that the ability to create and maintain trust is one, if not the most, important ability of executive leaders today (Barney & Hansen, 1994; Bennis, 1989; Butler, 1991; Kouzes & Posner, 1993).

Despite the widely recognized importance of organizational trust, it is a scarce commodity in organizations today. For example, in a recent internal study of a Fortune 500 industrial company, the employees were surveyed to learn if they trusted the firm's leaders to honor their value statement, which emphasizes "hard" (e.g., profitability) and "soft" (e.g., integrity and respect) values. Notably, more than half of the employees (55%) did not trust those in leadership positions to live consistently with the soft values, cynically believing that profits are the only thing that matters to those in power. According to a consultant who specializes in employee attitude surveys, the proportion of employees who did trust top management is uncommonly high even though it is less than half the employees of the firm (Stewart, 1996).

Furthermore, in a recent survey by Development Dimensions International, 56% of nonmanagement employees in 57 service and manufacturing organizations viewed lack of trust as a problem in their organizations ("Survey Finds," 1995). And Warren Bennis notes that organizational trust is impossible to maintain when layoffs are imminent—a condition that confronts or is confronting the majority of our organizations today (Hodgetts, 1996).

When organizational mistrust is pervasive, the collective shadow looms large. Illustrating this fact, Jeanne Borei and John Pehrson (1995) discuss how the collective shadow blanketed an entire organization after an intensive and "successful" 3-day management retreat. In this particular retreat, new energy was released, interpersonal barriers dissolved, and organizational trust grew. However, as time passed after the retreat, this energy became dark and rather sinister, interpersonal barriers were once again erected, employees started to withdraw, and mistrust surfaced again. From this instructive case, we learn that organizational trust is an ongoing and powerful force within organizations, which grows and shrinks in proportion to the organization's collective shadow.

Organizational trust is cultivated by everyone in the organization, but it is particularly influenced by having trustworthy people in leadership positions. Leader trustworthiness is generated when the leaders are perceived as (a) being skilled and competent, (b) having integrity, and (c) exhibiting benevolence to others (Mayer, Davis, & Schoorman, 1995). The first condition is met when the executive leader possesses the technical skills and organizational and industry knowledge to make crucial decisions and guide essential activity within the firm. When leaders are competent, their behaviors and the results of their behaviors are consistent and reliable (McGregor, 1967). Furthermore, followers have faith and confidence that leadership "knows what they are doing." In other words, perceptions of competence are necessary to enable organizational members to trust their leaders and focus on their immediate set of challenges.

However, leader competence is not enough. Organizational members must also believe in the moral character or personal integrity of their leaders if they are to trust them. When the leader has integrity, he or she is less likely to behave in self-serving ways and more likely to function in a manner that benefits the entire organization (Block, 1993; Ouchi, 1981). In other words, executive leaders with integrity are less likely to take unfair advantage of their employees, and this generates trust (McGregor, 1967).

Finally, leaders must also be perceived as showing goodwill, or benevolence, toward others. When a leader is seen as being benevolent to others, then the followers are more likely to cooperate and align individual goals with organizational goals. Furthermore, benevolence suggests that the leader has some specific and personal relationship with the followers (and vice versa). When the leader is perceived as being benevolent, there will be more risk taking and innovative behavior on the part of the rest of the organization (Mayer et al., 1995).

Organizational Trust and Leader Trustworthiness

Trust is an abstract term with multiple meanings (Mayer et al., 1995). Definitions of trust range from levels of openness that can exist between two people to the extent to which one person can expect another person to act predictably and in good faith (Gabarro, 1978). Karen Hart's (1988) belief continuum is helpful in clarifying the concept of trust. Hart points out that trust and its synonyms are belief concepts and can be differentiated by the degree to which the belief

Exhibit 8.1 The Trust Continuum

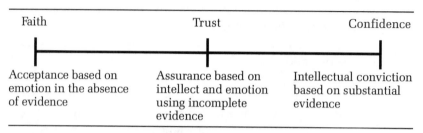

SOURCE: Hart (1988). Reprinted by permission.

is based on evidence. She explains that to believe is to accept something as true in the absence of full knowledge and that to believe in someone is to have faith and/or confidence that a person will not fail in their endeavors.

Because trust is a mixture of faith and confidence, Hart places trust at the center on a belief continuum bounded by these two concepts. Faith is described as an emotional belief that is based on little or no direct evidence. In contrast, confidence is an intellectual belief based on substantial direct evidence. Therefore, trust involves a leap of faith constrained by our confidence in previous evidence to be assured that others will act in a predictable fashion and with goodwill. This continuum is depicted in Exhibit 8.1.

If trust involves faith and confidence based on incomplete evidence, then organizational trust is a special context in which organizational members must develop faith and confidence in other members to help the organization function properly. Although trust is a characteristic of all relationships within a business enterprise, we are particularly interested in the perceived trustworthiness of its executive leaders because they model trustworthiness (or lack of it) and influence the context for all other organizational relationships. When the leaders are perceived as being trustworthy by their followers, then information flows smoothly and problems get solved (Bartolome, 1989), cooperation and coordination are enhanced (Barnard, 1938), turnover is reduced (Halverson, 1994), and innovation flourishes (Katz & Kahn, 1978). Indeed, recent theory argues that firms will have sustainable competitive advantages by having trustworthy leaders (Barney & Hansen, 1994), and preliminary research suggests that this is the case (Jones, 1997).

Barnes (1981) argues that leaders destroy trust when they operate under three common assumptions. First, they use either/or thinking exclusively and problems are framed so there are always winners and losers. For example, it is common for executive leaders to frame organizational problems in terms of union versus management, government versus business, theory versus practice, and us versus them. Either/or thinking forces people to take positions and creates an adversarial situation. It shuts down creativity and stifles dissent. Dogmatic either/or thinking reduces trust.

According to Barnes (1981), a second way that leaders destroy trust is when they operate under the assumption that "hard" data (e.g., financial and operating measures) are more important than "soft" data (e.g., morale and motivation). The hard-is-better-than-soft mind-set appeals to tough-minded executives, but it often creates mistrust. The reason for this is that trust is hard to measure, it is constantly changing, and it is situation-dependent. It takes intuition to notice conditions of trust/mistrust, and it is difficult to describe and communicate. Some executive leaders lack the ability or interest to learn about and cultivate this elusive skill.

Finally, leaders create mistrust when they operate under the rigid assumption that "nice guys finish last" (Barnes, 1981). Trust is usually reciprocal in nature, and if the organization's leader mistrusts members of the organization, this extreme mistrust is often replicated within the rest of the organization. This extreme but not uncommon view of how the world works can be deadly to organizational trust because it fails to balance cooperation and teamwork with individual initiative.

Trustworthiness of CEOs

Because leader trustworthiness is a perception or a belief made (and remade) by those who are led, a confidential survey was administered to the direct reports of CEOs (Jones & Judge, 1998). To get the broadest perspective possible, the most senior representatives from each of four functional areas (i.e., Production, Finance, Marketing, and Human Resources) were solicited for their views of the trustworthiness of their CEO. On average, three top management team members replied for each of the 56 CEOs involved in this phase of the study.

Exhibit 8.2 contains the aggregate responses to the 18 questions about leader trustworthiness. As can be seen from this exhibit, the CEOs were generally perceived as trustworthy by their immediate subordinates. Roughly 70% to 80% of the survey respondents indicated that their CEOs were trustworthy *fairly often* or *almost always* across a wide variety of behaviors that create or destroy trust. Indeed, nearly 70% of the respondents indicated that their CEOs almost always stayed "current in business matters"; and nearly 64% of them indicated that their CEO "demonstrates a good grasp of the firm's core competencies." These are clear indications that these followers see the CEO as competent. In sum, the data suggest that CEOs are generally perceived to be trustworthy, and the primary contributor to this perception is their well-developed *competence*.

CEOs were also perceived as having *integrity*, but their scores in this area were not as high as those for the competence measures. For example, only 57.7% of the respondents said that their CEOs were almost always to be "counted on to do what he/she has promised." Furthermore, only 39.2% said their CEOs were almost always "fair in making decisions." However, a majority gave their CEOs favorable ratings in these areas. These slightly lower scores suggest that the CEOs' integrity is more in question than is their competence.

Interestingly, the perceived *benevolence* of the CEOs was the lowest of the three sets of trust factors. For example, only 25% of the CEOs were viewed as almost always being "able to see both sides of an issue." Similarly, less than 28% of the CEOs were perceived as almost always demonstrating "concern for the best interests of others when making decisions." In general, CEOs are not perceived as being benevolent to others as much as having integrity and being competent.

On one hand, these results suggest that leaders are generally perceived to be trustworthy because all 18 measures of trustworthiness were favorably rated by their direct reports. On the other hand, the CEOs are perceived more as being competent than as having integrity. Furthermore, the perceived benevolence of the CEO was the factor that most limited his perceived trustworthiness. This implies that CEOs who are perceived to be competent, have integrity, and exhibit benevolence may be more effective in leading change than CEOs who only demonstrate one or two areas of trustworthiness.

Case Studies of CEOs' Views on Trust

In this phase of the research, I relied heavily on data collected by a former doctoral student of mine, Kathryn Jones. Kathy was interested

Exhibit 8.2   Top Management Team Members' Perceptions of CEOs' Trustworthiness ($N = 176$)

Trustworthiness Question: My CEO . . .	*Seldom or Rarely (%)*	*Once in a While (%)*	*Some-times (%)*	*Fairly Often (%)*	*Almost Always (%)*
1. Is candid in expressing how he feels about matters	0.6	2.8	9.1	28.4	59.1
2. Stays current in business matters	0.6	2.3	5.1	22.7	69.3
3. Looks ahead and forecasts what the future should be like	2.8	3.4	12.5	37.5	43.8
4. Is able to see both sides of an issue	1.1	5.7	23.9	44.3	25.0
5. Demonstrates a good grasp of the firm's core compe-tencies	1.1	1.7	6.8	26.7	63.6
6. Describes to others the kind of future that is desired	2.8	6.3	19.3	31.8	39.8
7. Makes rational and reason-able decisions	1.1	5.1	11.4	41.1	41.1
8. Brings new competencies to our team	3.4	6.3	20.1	37.4	32.8
9. Clearly communicates a posi-outlook for our future	1.7	4.6	9.1	32.6	52.0
10. Can be counted on to do what he/she has promised	1.1	2.3	9.7	29.1	57.7
11. Knows what he/she is talk-ing about when giving an opinion	0.6	2.8	7.4	41.5	47.7
12. Appeals to others to share his/her dream of the future as their own	4.6	9.1	15.4	31.4	39.4
13. Demonstrates concern for the best interests of others when making decisions	0.6	5.1	23.9	42.6	27.8
14. Is able to handle conflicts and stress effectively	2.8	8.0	15.9	42.0	31.3
15. Shows others how their long-term interests can be realized by enlisting in a common vision	4.0	12.5	17.0	35.8	30.7
16. Is fair in making decisions	1.1	1.7	14.2	43.8	39.2
17. Asks questions which go to the heart of the matter	1.1	4.0	7.4	33.5	54.0
18. Is contagiously excited and enthusiastic about future possibilities	3.4	5.1	17.0	27.3	47.2

SOURCE: Jones (1997). Reprinted by permission.

in learning more about leader trustworthiness, and she conducted in-depth interviews with CEOs and their direct reports for her dissertation research (Jones, 1997). As a pilot study, she interviewed the CEOs involved with this research study. Listed below are the results of her qualitative research on leader trustworthiness, which she was generous enough to share with me.

Role of Trust

Several CEOs indicated that when they are perceived as trustworthy by their subordinates, then the subordinates are more motivated to be productive. For example, Robert Masters stated, "It is hard to get people to be motivated without trust. I've got to be credible, have proper motives myself, and maintain my integrity to earn that trust. When I do this, the organization moves ahead." He also argued that "American society is too contractually minded" and that "trust fights this unfortunate tendency." He stated, "My word is my bond. We don't have employee contracts here, and we don't need them. Trust makes it all possible."

Others indicated that trustworthiness was essential because it enabled others to act in the absence of adequate information. For example, Steven Zolte was the leader of a firm that sold industrial products requiring an infrequent purchase cycle. He argued that he must be seen as trustworthy because if he isn't, employee turnover will increase and product quality will decline. Also, he believed that customers will be less likely to buy from the company if its leader is perceived to be untrustworthy.

Other CEOs emphasized the loyalty effect of trust. Joseph Henderson explained,

> Trust is very, very important. I have brought in three senior managers who have worked for me in the past, and a fourth is on his way. I believe that when you follow a leader to a new company, that is the ultimate declaration of trust in the relationship.

Most CEOs saw that trust starts with them behaving in a trustworthy fashion but that it needed to be reciprocated. This is particularly true in a decentralized organization that pushes decision making away from the apex of the organization. Randy Maxwell stated, "I have to trust in others to do the right things in order to decentralize. However, our employees have to trust me to do what is best for the company as well. It works both ways." Similarly, Richard Farr stated, "Trust is an important part of getting things done. The more I trust those who work for me, the more I can empower them. Without their trust, however, they will not follow."

However, some CEOs emphasized that they had to trust others and behave in a trustworthy fashion regardless of others' behavior. These CEOs were unconditional in their approach to others, and many did not see any alternative to this unilateral and unconditional approach. As Michael Breen stated, "If I don't behave in a trustworthy fashion, we simply won't survive. I have to trust and be trusted even when mistakes are made, decisions aren't thought out completely, and goals are not achieved."

Practices That Foster Trust

CEOs varied widely in the practices they pursued to create trust. For example, some CEOs concentrated on day-to-day interactions with their employees. These leaders focused on being honest in communications, keeping promises, handling information well, listening carefully, delegating thoughtfully, and being accessible. A typical response in this group came from Robert Masters:

> I have to be honest in all that I do. We have to pay our bills on time and encourage and practice teamwork. I must eliminate barriers to personal communication and try to reach as many people as I can at any one time. In particular, I must influence others who influence others—sort of a cascading effect of trust.

In contrast, other CEOs are more philosophical and rely to a greater extent on organizational systems in their approach to trust. These CEOs emphasize things like living by the golden rule and building that into company policies, creating and following the code of conduct within the firm, or keeping behavior consistent with the firm's mission statement. These CEOs avoid micromanaging their employees and seek to instill trust by creating systems and a culture of shared values. Joseph Henderson stated,

We have a company mission statement that revolves around quality. Employees sign it when they join the company, and management speaks about it every chance they get. We try to incorporate this mission statement in all that we do—hiring, promotions, work design, rewards—everything. Trust grows when we operate consistently with these principles.

Summing Up

The creation and maintenance of organizational trust is the paramount creative fruit of executive leadership. The presence of organizational mistrust suggests that the collective shadow is looming large and that leadership is deficient. Without trust, cooperation within organizations is not possible, and organizations are essentially a mechanism for cooperative activity (Barnard, 1938). Trust is a mixture of faith and confidence that others will behave in ways that are skillful and moral, with goodwill toward others. Consequently, executive leaders are viewed to be trustworthy to the extent that they are seen as being competent, possessing integrity, and exhibiting benevolence toward others.

Based on a general survey of direct reports to CEOs, we discovered that CEOs are generally viewed as trustworthy. However, their strongest trust-creating characteristic was competence, and their weakest characteristic was perceived as their benevolence toward others. This suggests that executive leaders who learn how to create a reputation for being competent, moral, and benevolent are unique and powerful leaders.

Despite the fact that all CEOs perceived organizational trust and their personal trustworthiness as being essential to effectiveness, their reasons varied considerably. Some saw the role of trust as being an important motivator of others; others saw it as enabling others to act in the absence of complete information; still others argued that trust instills loyalty and organizational commitment. Most CEOs saw trust as being a reciprocal process, but some saw it as a unilateral process.

There were two basic ways that trust was promoted within an organization by its executive leaders. One way was practical, detailed, and informal. This approach emphasized trust in the hundreds of day-to-day activities of the executive leader. In contrast, other executive leaders believed that a consistent and explicitly stated philosophy that was reinforced through formal organizational systems was the way to promote trust. In this case, trust was created and maintained through attention to the consistency of corporate values and behavior and constant communication with organizational members. Either way, the development and maintenance of trust was perceived to be a central and constant imperative of executive action.

Collective Shadow Work
With Organizational Trust

When the collective shadow of the organization is dark and oppressive, trust is rare. Chris Argyris (1986) explored this fact with his concept of "undiscussables." He indicated that when an executive in a leadership position sends out mixed messages, defensive routines emerge within the organization. These defensive routines enable employees to live with the mistrust and chaos created by mixed messages, but they also prevent the organization from investigating or eliminating the underlying problems. Suspicion grows, and people learn to live with inconsistencies that limit their effectiveness. In short, undiscussables must be explored by organizational members and their leaders if the collective shadow is to be addressed in organizations. Listed below are some questions to explore surrounding this issue.

Competence-Building Questions to Explore

1. Are there undiscussables in your organization? If so, what are they?
2. What organizational defensive routines have emerged to "protect" people from undiscussables?
3. What do *you* need to change to make undiscussables more discussable?
4. What is *your personal role* in perpetuating undiscussables in your organization?
5. What is the role of the leaders in perpetuating undiscussables in your organization?

Integrity-Building Questions to Explore

1. What are the mixed messages that you send out or receive within your primary organization?
2. Would you be willing to act in a way that fosters trust, even if it is not reciprocated?[1]

Benevolence-Building Questions to Explore

1. Who is hurt by undiscussables in your organization?
2. What can *you* do to end the harm done to others by discussing undiscussables?

Note

1. I am indebted to Kent Miller for this insightful question.

PART IV

Conclusions

Character and Creative Fruits Examined Together

Many leaders would rather have control than have access to more energy, devotion, and commitment on the part of the people in the organization. When leaders have to choose, they choose control.
— Roger Harrison, 1995, p. 164

The conventional view of leadership emphasizes positional power and conspicuous accomplishment. But true leadership is about creating a domain in which we continually learn and become more capable of participating in our unfolding future. A true leader sets the stage on which predictable miracles, synchronistic in nature, can and do occur.
— Joseph Jaworski, 1996, p. 182

Leadership always comes down to a question of character.
— Warren Bennis, 1997, p. 158

In earlier chapters, we focused on individual character issues and creative fruits of executive leadership. This approach allowed us to concentrate on the specific elements of the phenomenon we call leadership and its effects on the organization that is led. However, these character

161

issues and their creative fruits do not occur in isolation. In real life, they interact in complex and dynamic ways to yield the unfolding system we call executive leadership. In this chapter, we begin to examine the interrelationships between character and the creative fruits of leadership.

Character Integration

As Badaracco and Ellsworth (1989) argue, leadership is not about tailoring your "style" to a situation, it is more about being integrated within and living consistently with who you are. Thus, we begin our examination of interrelationships by exploring the relationships between personality preferences, personal values, and spiritual experiences of executive leaders. These three dimensions of character function like a three-legged stool: Each must be individually strong and supportive of the other two. In similar fashion, each dimension of character stands on its own and supports the other dimensions to make the leader more effective.

Because shadow work begins with initially coming to terms with one's personality, I will build my analysis around the personality types of these executives. Rather than examine all 16 personality types as was done in Chapter 3, I limited our examination to the four basic personality functions, or cognitive styles (Myers, 1993). These four functions or styles have received the most attention in the management literature, and they have been shown to reveal in a parsimonious manner many interesting and useful insights about executives (Walck, 1992).

Cognitive style refers to the manner in which individuals collect and process data. No style is inherently good or bad; however, each style has strengths and weaknesses associated with it. People with the intuitive-feeling (NF) style are known for their idealism and insightfulness into human systems. Their focus tends to be on new possibilities for people and on communicating those possibilities to others. Values are paramount in their decision-making processes, and these people work best in harmony with others (Lawrence, 1993). They rely on holistic, intuitive perceptions and generally maintain few decision-making rules (Haley & Stumpf, 1989), which some observers call a heuristic approach (Nutt, 1989).

People with the intuitive-thinking (NT) style also focus on new possibilities, but they rely much more on logic and impersonal analysis than on values to make their decisions. This style is particularly adept with new theories, concepts, and frameworks for ordering these new possibilities. This personality function (or cognitive style) can work without harmony and focuses on the generalizable principles involved with each situation (Lawrence, 1993). People with this style can be impersonal, and they may ignore "nay-sayers." Also, they often stress needs for innovation and risk taking (Haley & Stumpf, 1989), which some have called a speculative approach (Nutt, 1989).

The sensing-feeling (SF) style is the polar opposite of the NT style. People with this personality type enjoy applying what they have already learned through experience, seldom make errors of fact, and like to do things with a practical bent. They tend to look at the underlying values in the situation and feel rewarded when people's needs are met (Lawrence, 1993). They often concentrate on affective and evaluative parts of communication, and facts about people interest them more than facts about things (Slocum & Hellriegel, 1983). They often take a judicial approach to problems, which relies heavily on consensus (Nutt, 1989).

Finally, people with the sensing-thinking (ST) style are mainly interested in facts that can be collected and verified directly by the senses: seeing, hearing, touching, and so forth. They tend to make decisions by impersonal analysis through logical, step-by-step, cause-and-effect thinking. They are often very practical and skilled at collecting and analyzing the details of a situation (Lawrence, 1993). They prefer to compare options by using quantitative criteria and base their decisions on the findings of the analysis. They are often quite systematic in their approach to decision making (Nutt, 1989)

Because a considerable number (40 of the 91 or 44%) of the responding executives did not provide information about their personality, this analysis is somewhat incomplete. In the interest of completeness, I included these CEOs as a fifth column in each of the exhibits in this chapter even though I was not able to identify their personality type or cognitive style. Although this is suboptimal, it is a more comprehensive analysis and helps to remind us that there are many unknowns about the inner workings of CEO character.

Exhibit 9.1 CEOs' Top Five Terminal Values by Cognitive Style ($N = 91$)

Terminal Value	NF Type (n = 8) (%)	NT Type (n = 26) (%)	SF Type (n = 5) (%)	ST Type (n = 12) (%)	Unknown Type (n = 40) (%)
1. Sense of accomplishment	88	89	**100**	83	77.5
2. Family security	50	65	60	**83**	62.5
3. Self-respect	**75**	54	40	**75**	42.5
4. Salvation	50	38	40	42	30
5. Happiness	**50**	38	40	50	35
6. Wisdom	38	42	40	**50**	35
7. Freedom	25	23	20	17	50
8. An exciting life	**50**	35	20	25	20
9. A comfortable life	25	15	40	33	32.5
10. Mature love	12	27	20	8	15
11. True friendship	0	**27**	0	17	25
12. Inner harmony	0	19	0	8	25
13. A world at peace	13	0	**40**	0	20
14. National security	13	4	0	0	7.5
15. Social recognition	13	4	0	0	2.5
16. Equality	0	8	**20**	0	5
17. A world of beauty	0	8	0	0	5
18. Pleasure	0	4	**20**	0	0

NOTE: Highlighted percentages indicate that this personality type put that value in the top five values by a margin of 10% or more of its members, compared to all remaining personality types.

Personality and Terminal Values

Exhibit 9.1 examines the relationship between each CEO's top five terminal values and his personality function or cognitive style. The percentages indicate the frequency with which executives of that particular personality type selected that particular value as one of their top five personal values. By comparing the frequency distributions across the various types of personalities, we can begin to explore the propensity for certain values being associated with certain personality types. Furthermore, values that are particularly popular with certain personality types are highlighted in bold to indicate unusual attraction for that particular value.

For example, note that CEOs operating with NF and ST cognitive styles were more likely to emphasize self-respect as a preferred terminal value than CEOs with NT and SF styles. This finding is interesting as these types are, psychologically speaking, polar opposites of each other; it suggests that personality may not be the primary or sole influence of personal value preferences.

There are also some distinctive associations between personality type and terminal values. For example, NF executives were alone in their attraction to having an exciting life when compared to all other executives. In contrast, NT executives were much more likely to select true friendship and happiness as a favorite terminal value. Our minority group SF executives were the most distinctive with their emphasis on a sense of accomplishment, a world at peace, equality, and pleasure. Finally, ST executives were more likely to select family security and happiness as a favorite personal value than all other personality types.

Several of these interrelationships are consistent with personality type theory. For example, the ST executive is the most responsible and security-minded of personality types (Pedersen, 1993), so the selection of family security is not surprising. Also, the SF executive is oriented to justice and consensus (Nutt, 1989), consequently their selection of a world at peace and equality is expected. Furthermore, the NF executive is especially prone to becoming bored quickly with routine (Hirsch & Kummerow, 1990), hence the desire to have an exciting life is not surprising.

However, there are some unexpected relationships in this exhibit. For example, NT executives are not known for their ability to make or maintain friends (Pedersen, 1993), so their selection of true friendship was surprising. Similarly, people with the SF orientation have often been known to be less task oriented in order to focus on interpersonal relations (Corlett & Millner, 1993). As a result, it is surprising that all of the SF executives listed a sense of accomplishment as one of their top five personal values. Finally, NF types are often known for their social idealism and concern for others' well-being whereas ST types are known for their self-effacing sense of duty to others (Hirsch & Kummerow, 1990). Consequently, it was not expected that these executives would emphasize self-respect more than the other personality types.

One possible explanation for these unexpected findings is that there is some unknown third variable that influences these relationships. For this book, the context surrounding these CEOs—their demographic characteristics or the competitive situation—would be a prime area to consider. For example, it may be that the age of the CEO influences value preferences in combination with his personality. Alternatively, the CEO's spiritual journey may interact with his personality to influence his value preferences. We simply do not know how values are selected.

Another possible explanation for these unexpected findings is that the CEOs rate some terminal values because they are absent or diminished in their lives and they hunger for it more than other types. Relatedly, these executives may have begun to explore and work with their shadow energies; the selection of these values may reflect this movement toward wholeness. By becoming conscious of their non-preferred personality, these executives become whole in the full sense of the word (Bly, 1988; Johnson, 1986; Taggart & Robey, 1981). Selection of a previously nonpreferred part of their personality may be evidence of this process going on in these executives.

Personality and Instrumental Values

Exhibit 9.2 identifies how the selection of instrumental values and personality types interacts for these executives. As might be expected, the NF executives emphasized broadmindedness; the SF executives emphasized being helpful. These values are predicted by standard personality theory (Lawrence, 1993; Nutt, 1989; Taggart & Robey, 1981).

However, there are some unexpected value preferences that once again may suggest that conscious shadow work is going on or that unconscious urgings of the shadow are being expressed. For example, the NT executives emphasized loving over all other executives. Type theory predicts that these executives often have difficulties relating intimately with others (Hirsch & Kummerow, 1990) so this selection may be due to an unmet need that comes more easily to others. Also, the SF executives emphasized highly individualistic values, such as being responsible and capable and having self-control more than all other personality types. This might be expected for NT or ST executives, who tend to be highly individualistic, but not the SF executives, who tend to be the most oriented to group functioning (Hirsch & Kummerow, 1990). Finally, the ST executives emphasized being imaginative over all other types. Previous research has shown that imagination is some-

Exhibit 9.2 CEOs' Top Five Instrumental Values by Cognitive Style
$(N = 91)$

Instrumental Value	NF Type (n = 8) (%)	NT Type (n = 26) (%)	SF Type (n = 5) (%)	ST Type (n = 12) (%)	Unknown Type (n = 40) (%)
1. Honest	**100**	85	100	83	87.5
2. Responsible	75	73	**100**	67	77.5
3. Ambitious	63	46	50	58	45
4. Capable	25	46	**60**	33	37.5
5. Imaginative	38	38	0	**50**	40
6. Courageous	38	31	**60**	33	25
7. Broadminded	**50**	15	20	33	32.5
8. Logical	25	27	20	17	32.5
9. Independent	13	19	20	25	20
10. Loving	25	**35**	0	0	12.5
11. Self-controlled	13	23	**40**	25	12.5
12. Helpful	13	27	**40**	25	10
13. Intellectual	0	8	0	17	17.5
14. Forgiving	13	4	0	8	15
15. Cheerful	13	15	2	4	30
16. Polite	0	4	0	0	7.5
17. Clean	0	0	0	0	7.5
18. Obedient	0	0	0	8	0

NOTE: Highlighted percentages indicate that this personality type put that value in the top five values by a margin of 10% or more of its members, compared to all remaining personality types.

times pushed into the background as the ST executive drives to get the task done on time and under budget (Hirsch & Kummerow, 1990; Nutt, 1989).

Personality and Religious Affiliation

Exhibit 9.3 illustrates the religious affiliations broken out by personality type of the executives. We may recall that most of the respondents were from a Christian tradition, but there were some non-Christians

Exhibit 9.3 CEOs' Religious Affiliation by Cognitive Style (*N* = 91)

CEOs' Religious Affiliation	NF Type (n = 8) (%)	NT Type (n = 26) (%)	SF Type (n = 5) (%)	ST Type (n = 12) (%)	Unknown Type (n = 40) (%)
Christianity	100	80	100	100	95
Islam		4			
Judaism		8			2.5
None		8			2.5

in our survey. Interestingly, all of the respondents with known personality preferences who came from non-Christian traditions were of the NT personality type: 20% of these executives either aligned with some faith other than Christianity or were not part of some organized faith. This result is predicted by type theory as the NT personality type has been found to be the most independent and least conforming personality type (Myers, 1993).

Personality and Religious Orientation

Exhibit 9.4 examines the relationship between religious orientation and personality type. Interestingly, the SF executives were most likely to be intrinsically motivated to be religious as compared to the other types. In contrast, the NT and ST executives were more likely to possess an extrinsic-personal motivation for religious activity. Finally, the ex-

Exhibit 9.4 CEOs' Religious Orientation by Cognitive Style (*N* = 91)

CEOs' Religious Orientation	NF Type (n = 8) (%)	NT Type (n = 26) (%)	SF Type (n = 5) (%)	ST Type (n = 12) (%)	Unknown Type (n = 40) (%)
Intrinsic	38	27	**80**	45	20
Extrinsic-Personal	25	**42**	20	**42**	30
Extrinsic-Social	38	27	0	8	50

NOTE: Highlighted percentages indicate that this personality type was more religiously oriented for this orientation by a margin of 10% or more of its members, compared to all other personality types.

Exhibit 9.5 CEOs' Spiritual Experiences by Cognitive Style ($N = 91$)

CEOs' Spiritual Experience	NF Type (n = 8) (%)	NT Type (n = 26) (%)	SF Type (n = 5) (%)	ST Type (n = 12) (%)	Unknown Type (n = 40) (%)
I am very strongly religious/spiritual	38	38	40	**50**	20
I invest my time in daily religious/spiritual practices	38	39	40	**50**	25
I have felt some powerful spiritual force that seemed to lift me outside of myself	**50**	38	40	25	7.5
I feel extremely close to God	13	4	20	25	17.5
I have had an experience that has convinced me that God exists	75	58	60	83	60
I definitely agree with the statement: "God dwells within you"	**38**	27	20	17	27.5

NOTE: Highlighted percentages indicate that this personality type had a more intense spiritual experience by a margin of 10% or more of its members, compared to all other personality types.

ecutives with unknown type were most likely to have an extrinsic-social orientation toward religion.

Perhaps the most interesting finding is the strong intrinsic orientation of the SF executives. This finding is particularly noteworthy because the SF executive is the least common type to occupy the chief executive's position. Clearly, something unique is going on with these executives. One possible explanation for this result is that these executives draw substantive inner strength from their religious and spiritual paths to overcome the institutional biases against their personality type attaining the CEO role. Another possible explanation for this result is that SF personalities are inherently more intrinsically motivated in all of life, not just their religious life. Whatever the reason, this relationship is intriguing and worth further study and discussion.

Personality and Spiritual Experiences

Exhibit 9.5 reveals how self-reported spiritual experiences are distributed among the four cognitive styles. Notably, the ST executives reported the strongest commitment to certain religions/spiritual paths and to daily religious/spiritual practices. In contrast, the NF executives reported the strongest awareness of inner and outer spiritual forces. Both NF and ST executives reported the most frequent personal experiences of what they knew to be God.

These results suggest that executives with the NF personality type are the most likely to have had intense and/or memorable spiritual experiences whereas ST executives are the most likely to be committed to some established religious tradition. These results are consistent with personality type research, which has found the traditional forms of Christianity to be dominated by sensing types (Carskadon, 1981) whereas the more nontraditional forms of Christianity tend to be dominated by intuitive types (Gerhardt, 1983).

Character and Creative Fruits Integration

Inner integration is not enough. The true leader must seek consistency between his character and that organization to achieve the creative fruits of leadership. Therefore, we next explore relationships between personality type and vision, stakeholder preferences, and strategic goals.

Personality and Vision Statement

Each CEO was asked if he had an explicit vision or vision statement that guided him and his organization. Most (75%) of our respondents indicated that they did have a vision and they provided it to us. However, roughly one quarter of the executives did not have an explicit vision of the future. Therefore, it might be interesting to see if there are personality differences between having or not having a vision.

Exhibit 9.6 depicts the presence or absence of a vision statement related to cognitive style. The ST executive was the least likely to have a vision: 33% of these executives did not have one. In contrast, the SF executive was the most likely to have a vision of the future: 100% of these executives indicated that they had one. Type theory predicts that intuitive executives, with their focus on the future and new possibilities (Lawrence, 1993), would be most likely to see the value in vision statements. This prediction is supported by the ST executives' lower

Exhibit 9.6 CEOs' Vision Statement by Cognitive Style ($N = 91$)

(%)Usage of a Vision Statement	*NF Type (n = 8) (%)*	*NT Type (n = 26) (%)*	*SF Type (n = 5) (%)*	*ST Type (n = 12) (%)*	*Unknown Type (n = 40) (%)*
We do have an explicit strategic vision for this organization	88.5	81	**100**	67	87.5
We do *not* have an explicit strategic vision for this organization	12.5	19		**33**	12.5

NOTE: Highlighted numbers indicate the personality type that is more likely to have an explicit strategic vision by at least 10% or more of its members, compared to the remaining personality types.

relative usage of vision statements, but it is challenged by the SF executives higher usage of vision statements.

Once again, something unusual appears to be going on with CEOs who have an SF cognitive style. Because the SF style is relatively alien in the executive suite, one can speculate that people with this personality type need to do things differently to "swim upstream." The creation and dissemination of vision statements may be one of the tools used by SF executives to function effectively in a world that expects NT styles of leadership.

Personality and Stakeholder Orientation

Recall that each executive was asked to allocate 100 percentage points according to his organization's relative emphasis on each of four primary stakeholder groups. These four groups were owners, customers, employees, and the local community(ies). If the executives' responses were equal across the four stakeholder groups, then they were listed as having a balanced orientation. If the executive responses were greater than 50% for the owner group, then they were listed as having an owner emphasis. This 50% classification rule was also applied to the customer emphasis and employee emphasis. When 40% or more was allocated to the customer and community each, those executives were classified as having an external emphasis. Finally, when 40% or

Exhibit 9.7 CEOs' Stakeholder Orientation by Cognitive Style
       $(N = 91)$

(%)CEOs' Stakeholder Orientation	NF Type (n = 8) (%)	NT Type (n = 25) (%)	SF Type (n = 5) (%)	ST Type (n = 11) (%)	Unknown Type (n = 42) (%)
Balanced	62.5	31	60	36	40
Owner emphasis	12.5	19		18	25
Customer emphasis	25	23			22.5
Employee emphasis		15	20		
External (community and customer)		4		9	7.5
Internal (owner and employee)		4	20	18	5

more was allocated to the owners and employees simultaneously, those executives were classified as having an internal emphasis.

After making these stakeholder classifications, I analyzed the personality types of the executives. Interestingly, the NF and SF executives were most likely to have a balanced orientation among the four stakeholder groups. Compared to the other personality types, the NT and NF executives were more likely to have a customer emphasis. And the ST and SF executives were more likely to have an internal emphasis compared to the other two types. (See Exhibit 9.7.)

These results suggest that executive personality may influence the organization's stakeholder orientation. Executives with a preference for the feeling function (NF and SF) appear to be most committed to the stakeholder perspective where there is an attempt to honor and balance various stakeholder concerns. This is consistent with type theory, where the feeling function is the one most oriented to achieving harmony in all external relationships (Lawrence, 1993).

Executives with a preference for intuition (NF and NT) appear to be most interested in maintaining a customer focus for their organizations. Because customer satisfaction is a relatively intangible and abstract concept when compared to the more tangible, front and center presence of employee and owner satisfaction, perhaps the powers of intuition are required for this orientation. Clearly, research is needed to learn more about this relationship.

Exhibit 9.8 CEOs' Strategic Goals by Cognitive Style ($N = 91$)

CEOs' Strategic Goal	NF Type (n = 8) (%)	NT Type (n = 25) (%)	SF Type (n = 5) (%)	ST Type (n = 11) (%)	Unknown Type (n = 42) (%)
1. Customer satisfaction	87.5	85	**100**	**100**	87.5
2. Profitability	62.5	65	60	64	70
3. Employee morale	62.5	54	**80**	64	59
4. Quality/price leadership	25	46	20	55	37.5
5. Innovation	37.5	35	20	27	15
6. Sales growth	**62.5**	23		27	27.5
7. Service to community	25	11.5	**40**	18	25
8. Company prestige	25	23	20	20	12.5
9. Assets and reserves	25	11.5	**60**	45	15
10. Market share	12.5	19		18	20
11. Equipment/plant modernization			**40**		15
12. Dividend payout		8			8

NOTE: Highlighted numbers indicate the personality type that is more likely to identify this strategic goal as "extremely important" by at least a 10% margin above all remaining personality types.

Executives with a preference for the sensing function (SF and ST) appear to be most interested in maintaining an internal emphasis (owner and employee). This is consistent with type theory also, as the sensing function is most oriented to practical, here-and-now realities (Myers & McCaulley, 1993). Owners and employees are perhaps the most tangible and obvious aspects to every business, so perhaps that is why these executives are drawn to this orientation more than other personality types.

Personality and Strategic Goals

Exhibit 9.8 reveals the relationships between the strategic goals of the organization and the CEO's personality type. Customer satisfaction was the No. 1 strategic goal identified by all CEOs; however, the SF and

ST executives uniformly and unanimously agreed that this was an extremely important goal. This suggests that the sensing function is particularly drawn to this goal.

In general, the SF executives tended to be associated with organizations that were more extreme in their views of goals than the organizations led by other types of individuals. For example, SF executives emphasized employee morale, service to the community, assets and reserves, and equipment/plant modernization more than any other type. In contrast, they tended to ignore or downplay the importance of sales growth, market share, and dividend payout compared to others. This suggests that SF CEOs either operate in different environments than the other CEOs or that they see the world in a fundamentally unique way.

The only other noteworthy distinction is that CEOs with NF cognitive styles tended to emphasize sales growth more intensely than the other CEOs. This suggests that these individuals are either drawn to or excel in high-growth situations. Previous research has found that the intuitive type is overrepresented in high-growth firms (Ginn & Sexton, 1989). This implies that NF types may be unusually entrepreneurial in the CEO's role.

Summing Up

The purpose of this chapter was to examine some of the interrelationships between the character and creative fruits of executive leaders. To illustrate some of the connections, we explored similarities and differences between cognitive styles and various other aspects of character and their creative fruits. For each personality type, there are distinctive sets of values, religiosity, spiritual experiences, organizational visions, and strategic priorities. Of course, the context within which this occurs further influences these relationships.

In general, the analysis reveals that many of these relationships are predicted by traditional personality-type theory whereas some relationships are counter to type theory. One of the possible explanations for these conflicting findings is that some executives are either subconsciously feeling the nudge of their inner shadow or that they are beginning to consciously appreciate the previously rejected aspects of their inner self. Another possible explanation for these conflicting findings is that we did not consider the context within which the CEO operates, and that context can influence the situation as well. Whatever the cause or context, it is clear that character and its creative fruits do not operate independently.

Collective Shadow Work
With Character and Creative Fruits

Effective shadow work enables one to be more integrated and whole. However, even if you begin to own your shadow, you still must contend with an organization that may or may not have started addressing its collective shadow. For lower level employees, power to influence the collective organizational shadow is usually quite limited. But for those in the top management team of the organization, there is an unusual opportunity to do some collective shadow work. If you are in some sort of leadership position and desire better integration between your inner character and the creative fruits of your organization, effective dialogue and the community building process are excellent ways to pursue this (Maynard & Mehrtens, 1993).

Most organizations alternate unconsciously between superficial relationships (i.e., pseudocommunity) and unresolved conflict and chaos (Peck, 1987). When an organization has a leader who wants more creativity, commitment, and innovation, then that leader is increasingly engaged in creating a goal-directed community in the workplace (Judge et al., 1997). When organizations function like communities, individuality and commonality are integrated, conflicts get resolved, innovation is enhanced, and leadership is shared (Nirenburg, 1993). Of course, this rather idyllic state is not possible all of the time, but it is possible to experience on an increasing basis, using the community-building process (Gozdz, 1993, 1995).

The technologies developed for effective dialogue and community building can be pursued through dialogue groups (Bohm, 1990), community-building retreats (Peck, 1987), or both. These technologies require dedicated time away from office demands to examine the task and process of working together. Trained facilitators are available and are recommended to guide work groups through this rather intense and highly personal organizational development process. These technologies are not therapy groups; however, strong emotions are not uncommon in these settings. The investment in this process pays many dividends in increasing individual and organizational consciousness of their respective shadows and can lead to shared leadership.

10

Going Into the Shadow
and Emerging a Leader

Knowing ignorance is strength. Ignoring knowledge is sickness.
— Lao Tsu, translated by Feng & English, 1972, p. 71
(used with permission of Random House)

Keep walking, though there is no place to get to.
Don't try to see through the distances.
That's not for human beings. Move within,
But don't move the way fear makes you move.
— Rumi, translated by Moyne & Barks, 1986, p. 20
(used with permission of Threshold Books)

We need to remember that character, like a photograph, develops
in darkness. But then how can we follow our destiny when we
don't know what it is, when it's hidden in darkness?
— Robin Robertson, 1997, p. 3

The primary contribution of this book is to focus on leadership as an inward developmental journey of being that goes hand in hand with the more traditional views of leadership, which focus on what leaders "do" in their external world. Building on the revolutionary insights of

Carl Jung (1933), I used the metaphor of the human shadow throughout this book to guide and instruct the reader on this journey. Journeying into the shadowlands highlights the importance of seeking to become whole *before* assuming a position of leadership. However, sometimes the journey does not begin until after the leadership position is assumed. If this is the case, this journey is especially urgent, as it may help to avoid the harm that is created by those who are unconsciously wielding power. Although one's shadow work is never completed, a shadow is much less harmful when the executive is aware of its internal power and influence. As Warren Bennis and Burt Nanus (1985) noted, "The management of self is critical. Without it, leaders may do more harm than good. Like incompetent physicians, incompetent managers can make people sicker and less vital" (p. 56).

In this final chapter, I distill some of my earlier arguments; then, I discuss several implications of these ideas. One of the first implications is a new view on the leader's currency, which is power. Next, I highlight the importance of beginning shadow work before assuming a leadership role and offer some ideas on the unique challenges of starting to do shadow work while occupying a leadership position. Finally, I conclude with a discussion of the considerable benefits of doing shadow work.

Review of Earlier Points

Leadership is the act of consciously and creatively serving some greater good while empowering followers to become leaders themselves. Traditional literature on leadership emphasizes the doing aspects of leadership, using power to influence others. Although influencing others is unquestionably a part of leadership, this is a dangerously incomplete perspective. The traditional leadership literature misses the inner aspects, or consciousness, of the leaders (Bennis & Nanus, 1985; Quinn, 1996), what I call the "being" aspect of assuming a leadership role. Furthermore, it fails to recognize that leadership is inherently a creative act that empowers its followers; the absence of creativity and empowerment indicates the absence of true leadership.

To correct this error, leaders should focus on developing their character. Character is our inner structure of being that guides our perceptions and actions. To begin our exploration of character, we first focused on the context in which we operate. Context provides the challenges and opportunities for our character to grow and develop. For a leader, knowing the organizational and environmental context is the essential place to start before leading. Perhaps this explains why so many executive leaders are effective in one context but ineffective in other contexts (Goss, 1996).

Character is composed of three interrelated dimensions: personality, personal values, and spirituality. Exploration and knowledge of these three dimensions are essential to being a person of high character. Ignorance or neglect of our character does harm to us and those who come into contact with us. Leaders who ignore matters of character do harm to themselves, their followers, and their organizations.

Because the act of leadership is inherently creative, the evidence of leadership is its creative fruits. When leadership is present, the people in the organization are inspired by a shared vision of the future, operate with a common set of strategic priorities, and trust others in the organization (particularly those in leadership positions) to show them the way. When all three of these creative fruits are present, the leadership is particularly strong and effective. When some or none of these creative fruits are present, then the leadership needs to "reinvent" itself (Goss, 1996) or undergo "deep change" (Quinn, 1996).

The person who currently occupies a leadership position operates with varying degrees of awareness of his inner state of being. To illustrate this fact, I surveyed many CEOs in a wide variety of organizations and industries and documented their personalities, personal values, and spiritual understandings, as well as their visions of the future and strategic priorities. In addition, a colleague and I surveyed members of the top management team who report directly to those CEOs. Our goal was to learn about the perceived trustworthiness of their CEO and about the nature of their relationships with him. These two sets of survey data provided a broad perspective on the character and creative fruits of those in leadership positions and revealed that character and creative fruits come in many shapes and sizes. The data also show that leaders are concerned with these matters.

Complementing this broad range of survey data, I also included the results of personal interviews with seven CEOs to provide in-depth perspectives on these issues. Although not as comprehensive, these data make our exploration more human and, hence, more accessible. Their stories bring these issues to life, and the anecdotes offer a richer texture than the survey results alone. In particular, we catch glimpses of the shadows of these men as they candidly disclose their respective personal and leadership journeys.

Because shadow work involves intimate and deeply personal contact with that which is unconsciously rejected, it was not possible to conduct surveys or interviews with the CEOs about their shadows. However, the personal histories in this book move us closer to their inner experiences than previous research and make us more conscious and aware of the forces within. To paraphrase an old saying: "It is not what you know that can hurt you, it is what you don't know that does you in." All of us have a responsibility and an opportunity to explore and work with our shadows; this responsibility is particularly important for those in leadership positions because they have the power to be beacons of light or blankets of darkness on their organizations.

A Modified View of Power

One cannot do justice to the concept of leadership and leadership development without considering the concept of power as well. Traditionally, there has been an assumption that leaders have an ability to force others to do their will—and this constitutes power. But as we shall see, this is a narrow and distorted perspective on the power of leaders. Consequently, in this section, I offer a new view of power within the context of the leader's shadow.

Kenneth Boulding (1989) offers some of the most profound and recent ideas on power in the social sciences, and his ideas dovetail well with this book. Boulding defines individual power as "the ability to get what you want" (p. 15); however, he is quick to add that the notions of who you are and what you want are wide open. He goes on to point out that there are three basic forms of power (i.e., destructive, productive, and integrative), and each form of power has healthy and unhealthy applications. He concludes by arguing that all three forms of power are necessary to ensure the future of human civilization.

In many ways, leaders hold the key to the future of human civilization, as they wield tremendous power in their ability to get what they want through the organized efforts of others. Without conscious awareness of their shadows, leaders will wield this power unconsciously, which can lead to great harm. With conscious awareness of their shadows, leaders can destroy life-limiting entities, show the way for life-giving and productive organizations, and operate in a more integrated fashion.

Shadow work begins by challenging your identity and ends by refining what you truly want. Those who have not done shadow work are unconsciously controlled by their shadows, and these people often do great harm to themselves and their followers. In contrast, those who are aware of and who are working with their shadows are more likely to use their power in a life-giving manner. Destruction is sometimes called for, but the desire to destroy is not motivated by illusory rationalizations and/or imagined blame. Production is best enhanced, not through fear of retribution or desire for approval, but because of a deeper knowing of how things work and the right thing to do. The leader consciously engaged with his shadow is more personally integrated; this integration allows him to facilitate the integration of his top management team, organization, and environment. In other words, shadow work revises your concept of who you are and what you want so it redirects how and where power is used. Perhaps this is why "personal mastery" is central to system optimization (Senge, 1990).

The Special Difficulty of Shadow Work for Leaders

Anthony DeMello (1990) asserts that the three most difficult things for a human being to do are: (a) return love for hate, (b) include the excluded, and (c) admit you are wrong (p. 59). The major reason these three acts are so difficult is that they all involve transcendence of our shadows. Clearly, shadow work is difficult for all human beings.

However, shadow work is particularly difficult for those in leadership positions. There are four basic reasons for this. First, followers often make heroic projections onto their leaders (Johnson, 1991; Sonnenfeld, 1988). These projections are powerful and seductive for followers and leaders alike. Without awareness of this dynamic, leaders often feel compelled to live up to a projected heroic mythology rather than live out their own truth and circumstance. This is a key reason why self-authorizing leaders are so rare (Quinn, 1996).

Relatedly, shadow work involves dealing with the rejected parts of oneself; it is often perceived as "evil" (Zweig & Abrams, 1990). Heroes, by definition, are people who stand up for the "good" in life. Heroes are often perceived as pure of heart and mind. In contrast, shadow work forces one to recognize that we all have flaws—it is a very humbling learning experience that emphasizes the light and dark in all of us. Sam Keen (1990) describes this difficulty particularly well:

> The most terrible of all moral paradoxes, the Gordian knot that must be unraveled if history is to continue, is that we create evil out of our highest ideals and most noble aspirations. We so need to be heroic, to be on the side of God, to eliminate evil, to clean up the world, to be victorious over death, that we visit destruction and death on all who stand in the way of our heroic historical destiny. (pp. 202-203)

The second reason why shadow work is particularly difficult for leaders is because it often involves surrender and giving up the illusion of being in control (Zweig & Abrams, 1990). The chaos and messiness of shadow work do not fit with our notion of an orderly universe, particularly for the leaders who are "in charge" of dealing with a slice of that universe. Shadow work requires that we hold the tension of our opposites and wait for a creative response to surface in its own time and own way. This approach does not fit with our view of "strong" leaders, who act quickly and decisively in every situation.

Third, every leader has to deal with issues of unity and motivation. As Machiavelli argued, there are only two basic ways for a leader to motivate and unify a group, through fear or love. Recognizing this fact, many leaders too often rely on fear because it works quickly and pre-dictably (in the short run). For example, many leaders seek to vilify entities outside their group or organization in order to unify it within (Bennis, 1997). By creating enemies, we often project our shadow onto others and fail to develop our own character. Alternatively, many lead-ers use fear to move their subordinates in predetermined ways (Ryan & Oestrich, 1991).

Due to the enormous pressures to avoid one's shadow when in a leadership position, the prudent course of action is to learn as much as possible about one's shadow *before* assuming a leadership role. Of course, this approach will not eliminate the need for further shadow work when acting as a leader because some aspects of shadow work may not become apparent until one steps into a leadership position. However, it will enable leaders to be more effective and do less harm to themselves and others. Thus, shadow work is a continuous endeavor, but it gets much easier to do when one does it prior to assuming major responsibilities.

Perhaps this is why the CEOs interviewed in this book who had confronted the despair created by the Vietnam war, a bitter divorce, a job dismissal, or the specter of bankruptcy identified less with being "the leader" of their organizations and more as being on a spiritual journey. Each person confronted these low points prior to assuming the leadership role and became a stronger person for it. Ironically, these low points became the source of their power and leadership abilities. Such is the paradoxical quality of dealing with polarities and our shadow.

The fourth and final reason why it is especially difficult is because leaders tend toward extroversion (in North America), and extroverts find it especially difficult to go within themselves and wrestle with these inner challenges (Palmer, 1994). Recall in Chapter 3, we discovered that more than 7 of 10 CEOs surveyed were extroverts. This is not to suggest that introverts are any better at shadow work, it just means that the doorway to this work is less obvious and familiar to extroverts.

Recognizing Your Shadow

Recognizing one's shadow is subtle and difficult work—indeed, some would argue that it is the hardest work that one can undertake. Connie Zweig and Jeremiah Abrams (1990) pointed out that

> The goal of shadow-work—to integrate the dark side—cannot be accomplished with a simple method or trick of the mind. Rather, it is a complex, ongoing struggle that calls for great commitment, vigilance, and the loving support of others who are traveling a similar road. Owning your shadow does not mean gaining enlightenment by banishing the dark, as some Eastern traditions teach. Nor does it mean gaining endarkenment by embracing the dark, as some practitioners of black magic or Satanism teach. Instead, it involves a deepening and widening of consciousness, an ongoing inclusion of that which was rejected. (p. 271)

Similarly, Badaracco and Ellsworth (1989) argue that "leadership in a world of dilemmas is not, fundamentally, a matter of style, charisma, or professional management technique. It is a difficult quest for integrity" (p. 209).

Although there is no technique that assists in shadow work, there are several guidelines that help us achieve integrity and expand the awareness of our shadow. First, we need to recognize that often what we thought the environment was doing to us is really something we were doing to ourselves (Wilbur, 1990). Thus, we need to recognize that we are responsible for owning our shadow and limiting its harm—it is not "out there" victimizing us. Second, as Zweig and Abrams (1990) point out, the loving support of others who are traveling a similar road can be of great help. The journey can be lonely, and companionship and shared experience can make a difference. In addition, identify your most hated enemies and most admired heroes and explore the possibility that this is your shadow at work. Furthermore, be gentle with yourself. Shadow work is hard work, and it does no good to "beat yourself up" in the process.

If there is one technique associated with successful shadow work, it would be the pursuit of paradox. Robert Johnson (1991) argues, "Paradox has everything to do with the shadow, for there can be no paradox—that sublime place of reconciliation—until one has owned one's own shadow and drawn it up to a place of dignity and worth" (pp. 90-91). Similarly, Robin Robertson (1997) declares, "The shadow is paradox. While it initially appears to us as loathsome and despicable, it actually contains all our future potentialities for development" (pp. 137-138). It is very uncomfortable for human beings to stay with the clash of opposites. We want one side of the conflict to win out or for the conflict to go away through compromise. However, when two "truths" collide with each other and their reconciliation is not rushed, a new truth, a higher truth, replaces the previous truths; the conflict fades away. In sum, embrace the inner journey, particularly when it leads to paradox, for this is the way to recognize your shadow and become a more effective leader.

Benefits of Shadow Work

The benefits of shadow work are considerable and paradoxical. Central to this book is the premise that *those who are aware of their shadows and occupy leadership positions will do less harm and, there-*

fore, more good to themselves and their organizations. When a leader is aware of his shadow, he is more likely to act as a "servant" leader (Greenleaf, 1977) than as an autocrat. Recognizing his frailties and limits, he is less likely to burn out and go "stale in the saddle" (Miller, 1991) and more likely to function effectively as a team member (Sinetar, 1990). By making the "deep changes" that shadow work requires, he is more likely to help his organization survive and even thrive in the turbulent world in which we live (Quinn, 1996).

By touching our own death, we are given new life. Many who have taken this journey into the shadow lands report that they first feel like they are dying (Johnson, 1991; Zweig & Abrams, 1990). But if one can endure the experience of embracing the shadow, people often report having much more energy and a zest for life that did not exist previously. Indeed, much of what we repress in our shadows has been labeled "buried potential" (Zweig & Abrams, 1990), "hidden energy" (Signell, 1990), "our gold" (Bly, 1988), and even "contact with God" (Johnson, 1991).

Tracy Goss (1996) insightfully points out that "when you accept death, you are free to fully engage in life without compromise" (p. 96). Perhaps, this is one of the reasons the eulogy exercise used in Steven Covey's (1989) book is so effective. In *The Seven Habits of Highly Effective People*, Covey encourages all current and future leaders to envision and then write out their eulogy in advance of their death. By imagining the end of our lives, we begin to realize our time has limits. If we take these limits seriously (something that Americans find particularly difficult), these limits can be quite liberating. They force us to set priorities and encourage the development of "principle-centered" living. Without priorities and principles, life is an aimless, compromised wandering about. With priorities and principles, life is sharpened, creativity is enhanced, and the path one takes becomes more clear. Paraphrasing the twenty-third Psalm: "journeying into the valley of the shadow of death" brings new life.

Another paradoxical benefit of shadow work is that *by acknowledging the "evil" within us, the person often learns to accept him- or herself* (Wilbur, 1990). Jung (1933) argued that when one becomes conscious of his shadow, he also remembers that he is a human being like any other. James Hillman (1990) points out that when you love *all* of yourself, not just part of yourself, you are made free to fully experience life with all its twists and turns, triumphs and failures, hills and valleys. Paradoxically, by acknowledging the flaws and faults within us, we learn to accept ourselves more; and this self-acceptance leads to more compassion toward ourselves as well as others.

Finally, *leaders can move their followers to greater consciousness* (Bennis & Nanus, 1985), *but this is only possible if the leader has an expanded consciousness himself.* Leaders affect their followers most directly and their environments indirectly. If the leader is engaged with his shadow, he will be less likely to project his shadow onto others or allow others to project their shadows onto him. Being a role model of consciousness and inner awareness can empower his followers to learn from his example and become more responsible for their own lives. Ultimately, shadow work requires that we wake up and take responsibility for our lives. Effective leaders model this preferred path for others.

Although the benefits listed above are considerable and may entice some to engage their shadows, this listing is not meant to imply that shadow work is optional. Indeed, if you want to be whole, you must work with your shadow. The only choice is when to begin this work consciously. As Robert Johnson (1991) eloquently argues, "We must be whole whether we like it or not; the only choice is whether we will incorporate shadow consciously and with some dignity or do it through some neurotic behavior" (pp. 26-27). Conscious shadow work is painful and uncertain, but it brings life and vitality. Unconscious shadow work is also painful, and it brings with it a "slow death" (Quinn, 1996). As Zweig and Abrams (1990) put it, "We all have a shadow, or does the shadow have us?" (p. 3).

Throughout history, effective leaders have engaged their shadows, transformed themselves, and then provided developmental and growth opportunities for their followers. Some of these transformational leaders have become famous for their leadership skills, such as Mohandas Gandhi and Jesus of Nazareth, whereas others have operated less publicly. These leaders are people of rich character and extraordinary talent who understand and practice the concept of servant leadership (Greenleaf, 1977). Now that business organizations are arguably the most powerful institutions on earth, it is more important than ever that these organizations are led by men and women of character and integrity as well as skill in influencing others. This book sheds light on what is required of our current and future leaders. Great power brings with it great responsibility. It is the leader's responsibility to continuously engage his shadow so that organizations under his leadership will become healthier and more productive in the new millenium.

Appendix A:
The General Survey of CEOs

In early 1996, I mailed out a general survey to CEOs of publicly held corporations located in Tennessee, North Carolina, and Virginia to learn about their demographic and psychographic characteristics as well as some organizational attributes. This appendix provides details on that survey. Some parts of the survey are phrased in this section exactly as they were in the original survey. This text is in normal type. Other parts of the survey are paraphrased for brevity or I have noted their source in the literature. This text is in italics.

Personality Type:

Personality type was determined through self-reported previous MBTI results or having the respondents fill out Form G of the MBTI for the first time through a follow-up survey instrument. The MBTI is trademarked through Consulting Psychologists Press.

Personal Values:

These items were derived from Rokeach (1973).
Below is a list of 18 terminal values. Study the list carefully and select your five most important values. Then place a "1" next to the

value which is most important to you, a "2" next to the value which is
second most important, and so on until you have ranked your top five.

_____ A comfortable life (a prosperous life)
_____ An exciting life (a stimulating, active life)
_____ A sense of accomplishment (lasting contribution)
_____ A world of peace (free of war and conflict)
_____ Equality (brother/sisterhood, equal opportunity)
_____ Family security (taking care of loved ones)
_____ Freedom (independence, free choice)
_____ Happiness (contentedness)
_____ A world of beauty (beauty of nature and the arts)
_____ Inner harmony (freedom from inner conflict)
_____ Mature love (sexual and spiritual intimacy)
_____ National security (protection from attack)
_____ Pleasure (an enjoyable, leisurely life)
_____ Salvation (saved eternal life)
_____ Self-respect (self-esteem)
_____ Social recognition (respect, admiration)
_____ True friendship (close companionship)
_____ Wisdom (a mature understanding of life)

Below is a list of 18 instrumental values. Study the list carefully and
select your five most important values. Then place a "1" next to the
value which is most important to you, a "2" next to the value which is
second most important, and so on until you have ranked your top five.

_____ Ambitious (hardworking, aspiring)
_____ Broadminded (open-minded)
_____ Capable (competent, effective)
_____ Cheerful (lighthearted, joyful)
_____ Clean (neat, tidy)
_____ Courageous (standing up for your beliefs)
_____ Forgiving (willing to pardon others)
_____ Helpful (working for the welfare of others)
_____ Honest (sincere, truthful)
_____ Imaginative (daring, creative)
_____ Independent (self-reliant, self-sufficient)
_____ Intellectual (intelligent, reflective)
_____ Logical (consistent, rational)

_____ Loving (compassionate, affectionate, tender)
_____ Obedient (dutiful, respectful)
_____ Polite (courteous, well-mannered)
_____ Responsible (dependable)
_____ Self-controlled (restrained, self-disciplined)

Religious Beliefs:

Respondents were asked to circle their response to each of the following 14 items along a 4-point scale ranging from strongly agree *to* agree, disagree, *and* strongly disagree. *These items were derived from Allport and Ross (1967) and adapted to more religiously heterogeneous samples by Gorsuch and McPherson (1989).*

1. I enjoy reading about my religion. *(Intrinsic)*
2. I go to church because it helps me to make friends. *(Extrinsic-Social)*
3. It doesn't matter what I believe so long as I am good. *(Intrinsic reversed)*
4. It is important to me to spend time in private thought and prayer. *(Intrinsic)*
5. I have often had a strong sense of God's presence. *(Intrinsic)*
6. I pray mainly to gain relief and protection. *(Extrinsic-Personal)*
7. I try hard to live all my life according to my religious beliefs. *(Intrinsic)*
8. What religion offers me most is comfort in times of trouble and sorrow. *(Extrinsic-Personal)*
9. Prayer is for peace and happiness. *(Extrinsic-Personal)*
10. Although I am religious, I don't let it affect my daily life *(Intrinsic reversed)*
11. I go to church mostly to spend time with friends. *(Extrinsic-Social)*
12. My whole approach to life is based on my religion. *(Intrinsic)*
13. I go to church mainly because I enjoy seeing people I know there. *(Extrinsic-Social)*
14. Although I believe in my religion, many other things are important. *(Intrinsic reversed)*

Please check the religion that you are most closely affiliated with currently:

_____Christianity: _____

(please specify the denomination)

_____Judaism

_____Islam

_____Other: _____

(please specify)

_____No current religious affiliation

Spiritual Practices:

Respondents were told that there are no right or wrong answers to the questions below. Also, they were asked to check the response that is most true for them. These items, jointly known as the Index of Core Spiritual Experience (INSPIRIT) scale, were obtained from a study published by Kass et al. (1991).

1. How strongly religious (or spiritually oriented) do you consider yourself to be?

    _____Strong   _____Somewhat strong _____Not very strong

    _____Not at all   _____Can't answer

2. About how often do you spend time on religious or spiritual practices?

    _____Several times per day to several times per week

    _____Once per week to several times per month

    _____Once per month to several times per year

    _____Once a year or less

3. How often have you felt as though you were very close to a powerful spiritual force that seemed to lift you outside yourself?

    _____Never   _____Once or twice   _____Several times

    _____Often   _____Can't answer

People have many different definitions of the "higher power" that we often call "God." Please use your definition of God when answering the following questions.

4. How close do you feel to God?

___Extremely close   ___Somewhat close

___Not very close   ___I don't believe in God

___Can't answer

5. Have you ever had an experience that convinced you that God exists?

___Yes   ___No   ___Can't answer

6. Indicate whether you agree with this statement: "God dwells within you."

___Definitely disagree   ___Tend to disagree

___Tend to agree   ___Definitely agree

Background Characteristics:

1. What is your gender?   Male   Female

2. What is your current age? _____ Years

3. How long have you been working for this company?
_____ Years

4. How long have you been in the role as President/CEO?
_____ Years

5. Please provide a one sentence description of your vision for the organization:

Strategic Goals:

The following goals were listed, and the respondents were asked to indicate how important each goal is on a 5-point Likert scale ranging from not important at all to moderately important and extremely important. These goals were adapted from Bourgeois (1980).

Please indicate how important each of the following goals is to your firm:

1. Net profit

2. Rate of growth

3. Market share

4. Employee morale

5. Customer satisfaction

6. Company prestige

7. Innovation

8. Assets and reserves

9. Dividend payout

10. Quality/price leadership

11. Service to community

12. Equipment and plant modernness

Organizational Stakeholders:

These stakeholder groups were obtained from Judge and Krishnan (1994).
Each organization influences and is influenced by four stakeholder groups including owners, customers, employees, and the local community. Please indicate the relative importance of each of these stakeholder groups to your organization by distributing 100 points between them.

Owners:	_____ points
Customers:	_____ points
Employees:	_____ points
Community:	_____ points
Total:	__100__ points

Appendix B:
Field Interviews of CEOs

In-depth field interviews were conducted with seven CEOs who participated in the broader survey. I wanted to balance the general observations created by the survey data with in-depth insights created from one-on-one interviews. Each interview was conducted at the CEO's office and was audiotaped to ensure precision and facilitate subsequent content analysis. These tapes were then transcribed and analyzed to offer new insights into the inner life of executive leaders. Their stories are sprinkled throughout this book to offer specific details on how CEOs approach matters of character and creativity. To protect their identity, I have given them fictitious names and eliminated key facts and details that might allow the reader to determine who they are in real life. Below is the interview protocol that was used to conduct these interviews.

Opening Comments/Questions:

1. The reason why I am here is to learn about the inner experiences of being a CEO.
2. To capture your exact words and free me up to listen carefully, I would like to audiotape this conversation. Is that OK with you?
3. This information will be used for a research study on CEOs, but all the names and companies will not be disclosed in subsequent reports. Would you like to pick a pseudonym for you or would you like me to pick out one later?

Interview Questions:

1. Please tell me about your journey toward becoming a CEO.
2. Can you tell me what your most deeply held values are?
3. Please tell me about your spiritual journey.
4. Can you explain what your vision of the future is and how it was developed?
5. Please tell me what your strategic priorities are.
6. Please describe how you deal with conflicting stakeholder interests and strategic goals in your organization.
7. Do you have anything else to add about your inner experience as a CEO?

Closing Comments/Questions:

1. I plan to transcribe this interview and study it for patterns over coming months.
2. Would you care to see a copy of the transcript for your own records or to modify/elaborate on our conversation?
3. Thanks for your cooperation.

Appendix C:
Survey of Direct Reports to CEOs

To learn how trustworthy CEOs are perceived to be and what the impact of that trustworthiness is, Kathryn Jones (1997) surveyed the people who report directly to CEOs in publicly held firms located in the Southeast. She did this research to complete her doctoral dissertation work with me as the chair of her dissertation committee. Kathy was generous enough to share her data with me for this book. Below is the survey instrument that she used to obtain her data. These survey items were obtained and adapted from Kouzes and Posner (1995).

This section contains statements about various leadership behaviors and activities. Please read each statement carefully. Then, based on your knowledge of the decisions and actions of the CEO of your organization, rate the frequency with which each statement is true of your CEO. Using the scale provided, circle the number that corresponds with the frequency you have selected:

1. Rarely or very seldom
2. Once in a while
3. Sometimes
4. Fairly often
5. Very frequently or almost always

The CEO of our firm . . .

1. Is candid in expressing how he/she feels about matters.
2. Stays current on business matters.
3. Looks ahead and forecasts what he/she expects the future to be like.
4. Is able to see both sides of the issue.
5. Demonstrates a good grasp of the core competencies of our business.
6. Demonstrates to others the kind of future he/she would like for us to create together.
7. Makes rational and reasonable decisions.
8. Brings new competencies to our team.
9. Clearly communicates a positive and hopeful outlook for the future of our organization.
10. Can be counted on to do what he/she has promised.
11. Knows what he/she is talking about when giving an opinion.
12. Appeals to others to share his/her dream of the future as their own.
13. Demonstrates concern for the best interests of others when making decisions.
14. Shows others how their long-term interests can be realized by enlisting in a common vision.
15. Is fair in making decisions.
16. Asks questions which go to the heart of the matter.
17. Is contagiously excited and enthusiastic about future possibilities.

References

Abrahams, J. (1995). *The mission statement book: 301 corporate mission statements from America's top companies.* New York: Ten Speed Press.

Allport, G., & Ross, J. (1967). Personal religious orientation and prejudice. *Journal of Personality and Social Psychology, 5,* 432-443.

Argyris, C. (1958). Organizational health: What makes it healthy? *Harvard Business Review, 36*(6), 107-116.

Argyris, C. (1982). *Reasoning, learning, and action: Individual and organizational.* San Francisco: Jossey-Bass.

Argyris, C. (1986). Skilled incompetence. *Harvard Business Review, 64*(5), 74-79.

Autry, J. (1991). *Love and profit: The art of caring leadership.* New York: William Morrow.

Autry, J. (1994). *Life and work: A manager's search for meaning.* New York: William Morrow.

Badaracco, J., & Ellsworth, R. (1989). *Leadership and the quest for integrity.* Boston: Harvard Business School Press.

Balkin, D., & Gomez-Mejia, L. (1987). Toward a contingency theory of compensation strategy. *Strategic Management Journal, 8,* 169-182.

Barker, J. (1990). *The power of vision.* [Videotape]. Burnsville, MN: Charthouse International Learning Corporation.

Barna, G. (1994). *Virtual America.* Ventura, CA: Regal Books.

Barnard, C. (1938). *The functions of the executive.* Cambridge, MA: Harvard University Press.

Barnes, L. (1981). Managing the paradox of organizational trust. *Harvard Business Review, 59*(2), 107-116.

Barney, J., & Hansen, M. (1994, Winter). Trustworthiness as a source of competitive advantage. *Strategic Management Journal, 15,* 174-190.

Bartolome, F. (1989). Nobody trusts the boss completely—now what? *Harvard Business Review, 67,* 135-142.

Bass, B. (1990). *Bass and Stogdill's handbook of leadership: Theory, research, and managerial applications* (3rd ed.). New York: Free Press.

Baum, L. (1987, June 22). Corporate women: They're about to break through to the top. *Business Week,* pp. 72-88.

Beach, L. R. (1993). *Making the right decision: Organizational culture, vision, and planning.* Englewood Cliffs, NJ: Prentice Hall.

197

Behrman, J., & Levin, R. (1984). Are business schools doing their job? *Harvard Business Review, 62*, 140-147.

Bennis, W. (1989). *On becoming a leader.* Reading, MA: Addison-Wesley.

Bennis, W. (1990). *Why leaders can't lead.* San Francisco: Jossey-Bass.

Bennis, W. (1997). *Organizing genius: The secrets of creative collaboration.* Reading, MA: Addison-Wesley.

Bennis, W., & Nanus, B. (1985). *Leaders.* New York: Harper & Row.

Bertodo, R. (1991). The role of suppliers in implementing strategic vision. *Long Range Planning, 24*(3), 40-48.

Birchard, B. (1995, July). How many masters? *CFO Magazine,* pp. 49-54.

Block, P. (1993). *Stewardship: Choosing service over self interest.* San Francisco: Berrett-Koehler.

Bly, R. (1988). *A little book on the human shadow.* San Francisco: Harper & Row.

Bohm, D. (1990). *On dialogue.* Ojai, CA: David Bohm Seminars.

Bolman, L., & Deal, T. (1995). *Leading with soul: An uncommon journey of the spirit.* San Francisco: Jossey-Bass.

Borei, J., & Pehrson, J. (1995). Enter: The shadow. In K. Gozdz (Ed.), *Community building* (pp. 394-405). San Francisco: New Leaders Press

Boulding, K. (1989). *The three faces of power.* Newbury Park, CA: Sage.

Bourgeois, L. J. (1980). Performance and consensus. *Strategic Management Journal, 1,* 227-248.

Boyd, B. (1994). Board control and CEO compensation. *Strategic Management Journal, 15,* 335-344.

Breitenbach, J. (1989). Recruiting new board members. *Trustee, 42*(10), 14, 19.

Briner, R. (1996). *The management methods of Jesus: Ancient wisdom for modern business.* Nashville, TN: Thomas Nelson.

Brown, M. (1976). Values—A necessary but neglected ingredient of motivation on the job. *Academy of Management Review, 1*(4), 15-23.

Buchholtz, A. K., & Ribbens, B. A. (1994). Role of chief executive officers in takeover resistance: Effects of CEO incentives and individual characteristics. *Academy of Management Journal, 37,* 554-579.

Bunker, B., & Alban, B. (1997). *Large group interventions.* San Francisco: Jossey-Bass.

Burck, C. G. (1976, May). A group profile of the Fortune 500 chief executives. *Fortune,* pp. 65-68.

Butler, J. (1991). Toward understanding and measuring conditions of trust: Evolution of conditions of trust inventory. *Journal of Management, 17,* 643-663.

Carskadon, T. (1981). Psychological types and religious preferences. *Research in Psychological Type, 4,* 36-39.

Cavanaugh, G. (1976). *American business values in transition.* Englewood Cliffs, NJ: Prentice Hall.

Chaplains in the workplace. (1997). *Initiatives, 78,* 1.

Chappell, T. (1993). *The soul of a business: Managing for profit and the common good.* New York: Bantam.

Clarkson, M. (1995). A stakeholder framework for analyzing and evaluating corporate social performance. *Academy of Management Review, 20,* 92-117.

Cleland, K. (1994). Women daring marketers: Study. *Advertising Age, 79*(11), 28.

Collins, J., & Porras, J. (1994). *Built to last.* New York: Harper Business.

Collins, J., & Porras, J. (1996). Building your company's vision. *Harvard Business Review, 74*(5), 65-77.

Conger, J. (Ed.). (1994). *Spirit at work: Discovering the spirituality in leadership.* San Francisco: Jossey-Bass.

Corlett, E., & Millner, N. (1993). *Navigating midlife: Using typology as a guide.* Palo Alto, CA: CPP Books.

Cornell, B., & Shapiro, A. (1987). Corporate stakeholders and corporate finance. *Financial Management, 16,* 5-14.

Coulson-Thomas, C. (1992). Strategic vision or strategic con?: Rhetoric or reality? *Long Range Planning, 25*(1), 81-89.

Covey, S. (1989). *The seven habits of highly effective people.* New York: Simon & Schuster.

Covey, S. (1991). *Principle-centered leadership.* New York: Summitt Books.

Cowen, J. (1992). *The common table: Reflections and meditations on community and spirituality.* New York: Harper Collins.

Crosby, L., Bitner, M. J., & Gill, J. (1990). Organizational structure of values. *Journal of Business Research, 20,* 123-134.

De Pree, M. (1987). *Leadership is an art.* East Lansing: Michigan State University Press.

DeMello, A. (1990). *Awareness.* New York: Doubleday.

Donahue, M. (1985). Intrinsic and extrinsic religiousness: Review and meta-analysis. *Journal of Personality and Social Psychology, 48,* 400-419.

Donaldson, G., & Lorsch, J. W. (1983). *Decision making at the top: The shaping of strategic direction.* New York: Basic Books.

Donaldson, T., & Preston, L. (1995). The stakeholder theory of the corporation: Concepts, evidence, and implications. *Academy of Management Review, 20,* 65-91.

Drath, W. H. (1993). *Why managers have trouble empowering: A theoretical perspective based on concepts of adult development.* Greensboro, NC: Center for Creative Leadership.

Eichman, W. (1990). Meeting the dark side in spiritual practice. In C. Zweig & J. Abrams (Eds.), *Meeting the shadow* (pp. 134-137). New York: Tarcher/Putnam.

England, G. (1967). Personal values systems of American managers. *Academy of Management Journal, 10,* 53-68.

Fagenson, E. (1993). Personal value systems of men and women entrepreneurs versus managers. *Journal of Business Venturing, 8,* 409-430.

Fairholm, G. (1996). Spiritual leadership: Fulfilling whole-self needs at work. *Leadership & Organization Development Journal, 17*(5), 11-17.

Fairholm, G. (1997). *Capturing the heart of leadership: Spirituality and community in the new American workplace.* Westport, CT: Praeger.

Feng, G. F., & English, J. (Trans.). (1972). *Tao Te Ching.* New York: Vintage Books.

Fiegenbaum, A., Hart, S., & Schendel, D. (1996). Strategic reference point theory. *Strategic Management Journal, 17,* 219-235.

Fierman, J. (1990). Do women manage differently? *Fortune, 122*(15), 115-118.

Finkelstein, S., & Hambrick, D. (1989). Chief executive compensation: A study of the intersection of markets and political processes. *Strategic Management Journal, 10,* 121-134.

Finkelstein, S., & Hambrick, D. (1996). *Strategic leadership.* St. Paul, MN: West.

Finley, L., & Buntzman, G. F. (1994). What does affect company performance? *Arkansas Business and Economic Review, 27*(2), 1-11.

Fitzgerald, F. S. (1956). Letter. In E. Wilson (Ed.), *The crack-up* (pp. 65-78). New York: J. Laughlin.

Follett, M. P. (1942). *Dynamic administration.* New York: Harper & Brothers.

Fosberg, R., & James, J. (1995). Board rating changes and CEO compensation. *Managerial Finance, 21*(2), 12-23.

Fox, M. (1995). *The reinvention of work: A new vision of livelihood for our time.* New York: Harper.

Franz, R. (1998). Whatever you do, don't treat your students like customers! *Journal of Management Education, 22*(1), 63-69.

Freeman, R. E. (1984). *Strategic management: A stakeholder approach.* Boston: Pitman.

Freeman, R. E., & Gilbert, D. (1988). *Corporate strategy and the search for ethics.* Englewood Cliffs, NJ: Prentice Hall.

Friedrich, O. (1981, May 4). The money chase: Business school solutions may be part of the U.S. problem. *Time,* pp. 58-69.

Fuchsberg, G. (1990, June 6). Business schools get bad grades. *Wall Street Journal,* pp. B1-2.

Gabarro, J. (1978). The development of trust, influence, and expectations. In A. G. Athos & J. J. Gabarro (Eds.), *Interpersonal behavior: Communication and understanding in relationships* (pp. 290-303) . Englewood Cliffs, NJ: Prentice Hall.

Galen, M. (1995, June 5). Companies hit the road less traveled. *Business Week,* pp. 82-86.

Gallup Report. (1987). *Religion in America* (Report No. 259). Princeton, NJ: Author.

Gardner, W., & Martinko, M. (1996). Using the Myers-Briggs Type Indicator to study managers: A literature review and research agenda. *Journal of Management, 22,* 45-83.

Gerhardt, R. (1983). Liberal religion and personality type. *Research in Psychological Type, 6,* 26-29.

Ginn, C., & Sexton, D. (1989). Psychological types of Inc. 500 founders and their spouses. *Journal of Psychological Type, 16,* 3-12.

Godfrey, P., & Hill, C. (1995). The problem of unobservables in strategic management research. *Strategic Management Journal, 16,* 519-533.

Gorsuch, R., & McPherson, S. (1989). Intrinsic/extrinsic measurement: I/E-Revised and single-item scales. *Journal for the Scientific Study of Religion, 28,* 348-354.

Goss, T. (1996). *The last word on power: Re-invention for leaders and anyone who must make the impossible happen.* New York: Currency Doubleday.

Gozdz, K. (1993). Building community as a leadership discipline. In M. Ray & A. Rinzler (Eds.), *The new paradigm of business* (pp. 107-119). New York: Jeremy Tarcher.

Gozdz, K. (Ed.). (1995). *Community building.* San Francisco: New Leaders Press.

Grace, P. (1985). *Annual report.* Boca Raton, FL: W. R. Grace & Co.

Grant, L. (1996). Rambos in pinstripes: Why so many CEOs are lousy leaders. *Fortune, 133,* 147.

Greenleaf, R. (1977). *Servant leadership: A journey into the nature of legitimate power and greatness.* New York: Paulist Press.

Grube, L. (1995). CEOs at risk. *Chief Executive, 108,* 42-43.

Guth, W., & Taguiri, R. (1965). Personal values and corporate strategy. *Harvard Business Review, 43*(5), 123-135.

Haas, H. (1992). *The leader within: An empowering path of self-discovery.* New York: Harper Publishing.

Haley, U., & Stumpf, S. (1989). Cognitive traits in strategic decision making: Linking theories of personalities and cognitions. *Journal of Management Studies, 26,* 477-497.

Hallstein, R. (1992). *Memoirs of a recovering autocrat: Revealing insights for managing the autocrat in all of us.* San Francisco: Berrett-Koehler.

Halverson, R. (1994). The construct and measurement of the development of trust and respect in leader-subordinate relationships. *Dissertation Abstracts International,* B54(7), 3883. University Microforms Number AAC 9333537.

Hambrick, D., & Fukotomi, G. (1991). The seasons of a CEO's tenure. *Academy of Management Review, 16,* 719-742.

Hambrick, D., & Mason, P. (1984). Upper echelons: The organization as a reflection of its top managers. *Academy of Management Review, 9,* 193-206.

Hamel, G. (1998). Strategy innovation and the quest for value. *Sloan Management Review, 39*(2), 7-14.

Hamel, G., & Prahalad, C. K. (1989, May/June). Strategic intent. *Harvard Business Review,* pp. 63-76.

Hammer, A., & Mitchell, W. (1996). The distribution of MBTI types in the U.S. by gender and ethnic group. *Journal of Psychological Type, 37,* 2-15.

Harman, W., & Hormann, J. (1993). The breakdown of the old paradigm: Chapter 1. In M. Ray (Ed.), *The new paradigm of business* (pp. 16-27). Los Angeles: Tarcher.

Harris, M. (1991). *Sisters in the shadow.* Norman: University of Oklahoma Press.

Harrison, R. (1995). *Consultant's journey: A dance of work and spirit.* San Francisco: Jossey-Bass.

Hart, K. (1988). Kinship, contact, and trust: The economic organization of migrants in an African city slum. In D. Gambetta (Ed.), *Trust: Making and breaking cooperative relations* (pp. 176-211), New York: Basil Blackwell.

Hawley, J. (1993). *Reawakening the spirit in work: The power of dharmic management.* San Francisco: Berrett-Koehler.

Heller, R. (1990, February). Sins of omission. *Management Today,* p. 28.

Hellriegel, D., & Slocum, J. (1980). Preferred organizational designs and problem-solving styles. *Human Systems Management, 7,* 151-158.

Hill, C., & Phan, P. (1991). CEO tenure as a determinant of CEO pay. *Academy of Management Journal, 34,* 707-717.

Hillman, J. (1990). The cure of the shadow. In C. Zweig & J. Abrams (Eds.), *Meeting the shadow* (pp. 242-243). New York: Tarcher/Putnam.

Hirsch, S. K., & Kummerow, J. M. (1990). *Introduction to type in organizations* (2nd ed.). Palo Alto, CA: Consulting Psychologists Press.

Hodgetts, R. (1996). A conversation with Warren Bennis on leadership in the midst of downsizing. *Organizational Dynamics, 25*(1), 72-78.

Jacobs, R. (1994). *Real-time strategic change.* San Francisco: Berrett-Koehler.

James, W. (Ed.). (1878). *Familiar quotations by John Bartlett.* Boston: Little, Brown.

Jaworski, J. (1996). *Synchronicity: The inner path of leadership.* San Francisco: Berrett-Koehler.

Johnson, R. (1986). *Inner work: Using dreams and active imagination for personal growth.* San Francisco: Harper.

Johnson, R. (1991). *Owning your own shadow: Understanding the dark side of the psyche.* San Francisco: Harper.

Jones, K. (1997). *CEO trustworthiness: A universal or context-specific organizational advantage?* Unpublished doctoral dissertation, University of Tennessee, Knoxville.

Jones, K., & Judge, W. (1998). *CEO trustworthiness as a source of competitive advantage: A resource-based perspective.* Paper presented to the Business Policy and Strategy Division, National Academy of Management Meetings, San Diego, CA.

Jones, L. (1995). *Jesus—CEO: Using ancient wisdom for visionary leadership.* New York: Hyperion.

Jones, T. (1995). Instrumental stakeholder theory: A synthesis of ethics and economics. *Academy of Management Review, 20,* 404-437.

Judge, W., & Dobbins, G. (1995). Antecedents and effects of outside director's awareness of CEO decision style. *Journal of Management, 21*(1), 43-64.

Judge, W., Fryxell, G., & Dooley, R. (1997). The new task of R&D management: Creating goal-directed communities for innovation. *California Management Review, 39*(3), 72-85.

Judge, W., & Krishnan, H. (1994). An empirical investigation of the scope of a firm's enterprise strategy. *Business & Society, 33,* 167-190.

Judge, W., & Zeithaml, C. (1992). Institutional and strategic choice perspectives on board involvement in the strategic decision process. *Academy of Management Journal, 35,* 766-794.

Jung, C. G. (1923). *Psychological types.* New York: Harcourt Brace.

Jung, C. G. (1933). *Modern man in search of a soul.* New York: Harcourt Brace.

Kahle, L., & Kennedy, P. (1988). Using the list of values (LOV) to understand consumers. *Journal of Services Marketing, 2*(4), 49-56.

Kahneman, D., & Tversky, A. (1979). Prospect theory: An analysis of decisions under risk. *Econometrica, 47,* 263-291.

Kaku, R. (1997). The path of kyosei. *Harvard Business Review, 75*(4), 55-63.

Kallen, B. (1986, December 1). Praying for guidance. *Forbes,* pp. 220-221.

Kamakura, W., & Mazzon, J. (1991). Value segmentation: A model for the measurement of values and value systems. *Journal of Consumer Research, 18,* 208-218.

Kantrowitz, B. (1994, November 28). In search of the sacred. *Newsweek,* pp. 53-55.

Kaplan, R., & Norton, D. (1992). The balanced scorecard—Measures that drive performance. *Harvard Business Review, 70,* 71-79.

Kaplan, R., & Norton, D. (1996). Using the balanced scorecard as a strategic management system. *Harvard Business Review, 74*(1), 75-85.

Kass, J., Friedman, R., Leserman, J., Zuttermeister, P., & Benson, H. (1991). Health outcomes and a new index of spiritual experience. *Journal for the Scientific Study of Religion, 30,* 203-211.

Katz, D., & Kahn, R. (1978). *The social psychology of organizations.* New York: John Wiley.

Keen, S. (1990). The enemy maker. In C. Zweig & J. Abrams (Eds.), *Meeting the shadow* (pp. 197-203). New York: Tarcher/Putnam.

Kelley, R. (1992). *The power of followership: How to create leaders people want to follow and followers who lead themselves.* New York: Currency Doubleday.

Kilmann, R., & Saxton, M. (1991). *Kilmann-Saxton culture-gap survey.* Tuxedo, NY: Xicom.

Kofidomos, J. R. (1989). *Why executives lose their balance.* Greensboro, NC: Center for Creative Leadership.

Kotter, J. (1990). *A force for change: How leadership differs from management.* New York: Free Press.

Kotter, J., & Heskett, J. (1992). *Corporate culture and performance.* New York: Free Press.

Kouzes, J., & Posner, B. (1993). *Credibility: How leaders gain and lose it, why people demand it.* San Francisco: Jossey-Bass.

Kouzes, J., & Posner, B. (1995). *The leadership challenge: How to get extraordinary things done in organizations.* San Francisco: Jossey-Bass.

Kuhn, T. (1970). *The structure of scientific revolutions* (2nd ed.). Chicago: University of Chicago Press.

Kurtz, D. L., Boone, L. E., & Fleenor, C. P. (1989). *CEO: Who gets to the top in America.* East Lansing: Michigan State University Press.

Laabs, J. (1995). Balancing spirituality and work. *Personnel Journal, 74*(9), 60-76.

Larwood, L., Falbe, C., Kriger, M., & Miesing, P. (1995). Structure and meaning of organizational vision. *Academy of Management Journal, 38,* 740-769.

Lawler, J. (1994). Executive exodus. *Working Woman, 19*(11), 38-41.

Lawrence, G. (1993). *People types & tiger stripes* (3rd ed.). Gainesville, FL: Center for Applications of Psychological Type.

Leong, F., & Zachar, P. (1990). An evaluation of Allport's religious orientation scale across one Australian and two United States samples. *Educational and Psychological Measurement, 50*, 359-368.

Levinson, D. (1978). *Seasons of a man's life*. New York: Ballantine.

Lewis, H. (1990). *A question of values: Six ways we make the personal choices that shape our lives*. New York: Harper & Row.

Loden, M. (1987). Recognizing women's potential: No longer business as usual. *Management Review, 76*(12), 44-46.

Machan, D. (1989). Taking charge. *Forbes, 143*, 154-156.

Machiavelli, N. (1962). *The prince*. New York: Mentor Press. (Original work published 1513)

Marks, M. (1988, September). The disappearing company man. *Psychology Today*, pp. 34-39.

Maslow, A. (1954). *Motivation and personality*. New York: Harper & Row.

Mastony, C. (1998, July 27). Managing with God. *Forbes*, pp. 17-19.

Mayer, R., Davis, J., & Schoorman, F. D. (1995). An integrative model of organizational trust. *Academy of Management Review, 20*, 709-734.

Maynard, H., & Mehrtens, S. (1993). *The fourth wave: Business in the 21st century*. San Francisco: Berrett-Koehler.

McCabe, D., Dukerich, J., & Dutton, J. (1991). Context, value, and moral dilemmas: Comparing the choices of business and law students. *Journal of Business Ethics, 10*, 951-950.

McCall, M., Lombardo, M., & Morrison, A. (1988). *The lessons of experience: How successful executives develop on the job*. New York: Free Press.

McClenahen, J. (1991). Fear of succession. *Industry Week, 240*(20), 64.

McGregor, D. (1967). *The professional manager*. New York: McGraw-Hill.

Merriam-Webster. (1983). *Webster's ninth new collegiate dictionary*. Springfield, MA: Author.

Michel, J., & Hambrick, D. (1992). Diversification posture and top management team characteristics. *Academy of Management Journal, 35*, 9-37.

Miles, R., Coleman, H., & Creed, D. (1995). Keys to success in corporate redesign. *California Management Review, 37*(3), 128-145.

Miller, D. (1991). Stale in the saddle: CEO tenure and the match between organization and environment. *Management Science, 37*, 34-52.

Miller, D., & Toulouse, J. (1986a). Chief executive personality and corporate strategy and structure in small firms. *Management Science, 32*, 1389-1409.

Miller, D., & Toulouse, J. (1986b). Strategy, structure, CEO personality, and performance in small firms. *American Journal of Small Business, 10*(3), 46-67.

Mirvis, P. (1997). Soul work in organizations. *Organization Science, 8*(2), 193-206.

Mitroff, I. (1983). *Stakeholders of the organizational mind*. San Francisco: Jossey-Bass.

Mitroff, I., Barabba, V., & Kilmann, R. (1977). The application of behavioral and philosophical technologies to strategic planning: A case study of a large federal agency. *Management Science, 24*(1), 44-58.

Mitroff, I., & Kilmann, R. (1975, July). Stories managers tell: A new tool for organizational problem solving. *Management Review*, 19-28.

Moyne, J., & Barks, C. (Trans.). (1986). *Unseen rain: Quatrains of Rumi*. Putney, VT: Threshold Books.

Myers, I. B. (1993). *Introduction to type* (5th ed.). Palo Alto, CA: Consulting Psychologists Press.

Myers, I. B., & McCaulley, M. (1993). *Manual: A guide to the development and use of the Myers-Briggs Type Indicator.* Palo Alto, CA: Consulting Psychologists Press.

Myers, I. B., & Myers, P. B. (1993). *Gifts differing: Understanding personality type.* Palo Alto, CA: CPP Books.

Nahavandi, A., Malezadeh, A., & Mizzi, P. (1991, May/June). Leaders and how they manage. *Journal of Business Strategy, 12,* 47-49.

Nair, K. (1994). *A higher standard of leadership: Lessons from the life of Gandhi.* San Francisco: Berrett-Koehler.

Napier, N., & Smith, M. (1987). Product diversification, performance criteria, and compensation at the corporate level. *Strategic Management Journal, 8,* 195-201.

Needleman, J. (1991). *Money and the meaning of life.* New York: Currency Doubleday.

Nirenburg, J. (1993). *The living organization: Transforming teams into workplace communities.* New York: Irwin.

Norburn, D. (1986). GOGOs, YOYOs, and DODOs: Company directors and industry performance. *Strategic Management Journal, 9,* 225-237.

Northouse, P. (1997). *Leadership: Theory and practice.* Thousand Oaks, CA: Sage.

Novak, M. (1996). *Business as a calling: Work and the examined life.* New York: Free Press.

Novick, R., & Brown, D. (1995). The trouble with religion: An interview with Matthew Fox. *Sun Magazine, 232,* 8-15.

Nutt, P. (1989). *Making tough decisions.* San Francisco: Jossey-Bass.

Orts, E. (1992). Beyond shareholders: Interpreting corporate constituency statutes. *The George Washington Law Review, 61*(1), 14-135.

Oswald, S., Mossholder, K., & Harris, S. (1994). Vision salience and strategic involvement: Implications for psychological attachment to organization and job. *Strategic Management Journal, 15,* 477-489.

Oswald, S., Stanwick, P., & LaTour, M. (1997). The effect of vision, strategic planning, and cultural relationships on organizational performance: A structural approach. *International Journal of Management, 14,* 521-529.

Ouchi, W. (1981). *Theory Z: How American business can meet the Japanese challenge.* Reading, MA: Addison-Wesley.

Owen, H. (1993). *Open space technology.* Potomac, MD: Abbot Press.

Palmer, P. (1994). Leading from within: Out of the shadow, into the light. In J. Conger (Ed.), *Spirit at work* (pp. 19-40). San Francisco: Jossey-Bass

Peck, S. (1987). *The different drum.* New York: Simon & Schuster.

Pedersen, L. (1993). *Sixteen men: Understanding masculine personality types.* Boston: Shambhala Press.

Peters, T., & Waterman, R. (1982). *In search of excellence.* New York: Harper & Row.

Pollitt, I. (1982). Managing differences in industry. *Journal of Psychological Type, 5,* 2-13.

Pratt, N. (1996). CEOs reap unprecedented riches while employees' pay stagnates. *Compensation Benefits Review, 28*(5), 20-24.

Provost, J. (1990). *Work, type, and play: Achieving balance in your life.* Palo Alto, CA: CPP Books.

Quenk, N. (1993). Personality types or personality traits: What difference does it make? *Bulletin of Psychological Type, 16*(2), 9-13.

Quinn, J. B. (1980). *Strategies for change.* Homewood, IL: Irwin.

Quinn, R. E. (1991). *Beyond rational management: Mastering the paradoxes and competing demands of high performance.* San Francisco: Jossey-Bass.

Quinn, R. E. (1996). *Deep change: Discovering the leader within.* San Francisco: Jossey-Bass.

Ragins, B., Townsend, B., & Mattis, M. (1998). Gender gap in the executive suite: CEOs and female executives report on breaking the glass ceiling. *Academy of Management Executive, 12*(1), 28-42.

Ray, M., & Rinzler, A. (Eds.). (1993). *The new paradigm in business.* New York: Putnam.

Renesch, J. (Ed.). (1992). *New traditions in business.* San Francisco: Berrett-Koehler.

Reynierse, J. (1993). The distribution and flow of managerial types through organizational levels in business and industry. *Journal of Psychological Type, 25,* 11-23.

Richards, M. D. (1986). *Setting strategic goals and objectives.* St. Paul, MN: West Publishing.

Richardson, P. (1996). *Four spiritualities: Expressions of self, expressions of spirit.* Palo Alto, CA: Davies-Black.

Roach, B. (1982). Organizational decision makers: Different types for different levels. *Journal of Psychological Type, 12,* 16-24.

Robertson, R. (1997). *Your shadow.* Virginia Beach, VA: ARE Press.

Rokeach, M. (1973). *The nature of human values.* New York: Free Press.

Rokeach, M., & Ball-Rokeach, S. (1989). Stability and change in American value priorities, 1968-1981. *American Psychologist, 44,* 775-784.

Roof, W. R. (1993). *A generation of seekers: The spiritual journeys of the baby boom generation.* San Francisco: Harper Collins.

Roskind, R. (1992). *In the spirit of business.* Berkeley, CA: Celestial Arts.

Rutte, M. (1996, March). *Spirituality in the workplace.* Presentation for the International Association for Business & Society, Santa Fe, NM.

Ryan, K., & Oestrich, D. (1991). *Driving fear out of the workplace.* San Francisco: Jossey-Bass.

Rytting, M., Ware, R., & Prince, R. (1994). Bimodal distributions in a sample of CEOs: Validating evidence for the MBTI. *Journal of Psychological Type, 31,* 16-23.

Sanders, W., Davis-Blake, A., & Fredrickson, J. (1995, August). Prizes with strings attached: Determinants of the structure of CEO compensation. In *Academy of Management Best Paper Proceedings* (pp. 266-270). Victoria, BC: Academy of Management.

Schein, E. (1990). *Organizational culture and leadership.* San Francisco: Jossey-Bass.

Schmidt, W., & Posner, B. (1982). *Managerial values and expectations.* New York: American Management Association.

Schmidt, W., & Posner, B. (1986). Values and expectations of federal service executives. *Public Administration Review, 46,* 447-454.

Selznick, P. (1957). *Leadership in administration: A sociological interpretation.* Evanston, IL: Row, Peterson.

Senge, P. (1990). *The fifth discipline: The art and practice of the learning organization.* New York: Doubleday.

Sharplin, A. (1994). *The Lincoln Electric Company.* New York: North American Case Research Association.

Sherman, S. (1994). Leaders learn to heed the voice within. *Fortune, 130*(4), pp. 92-100.

Shipka, B. (1997). *Leadership in a challenging world: A sacred journey.* Boston: Butterworth-Heineman.

Shoemaker, P. (1997). Disciplined imagination: From scenarios to strategic options. *International Studies of Management and Organization, 27*(2), 43-70.

Signell, K. (1990). Working with women's dreams. In C. Zweig & J. Abrams (Eds.), *Meeting the shadow* (pp. 256-259). New York: Tarcher/Putnam.

Sinetar, M. (1987). *Do what you love: The money will follow.* New York: Dell.

Sinetar, M. (1990). Using our flaw and faults. In C. Zweig & J. Abrams (Eds.), *Meeting the shadow* (pp. 116-118). New York: Tarcher/Putnam.

Singer, A. E. (1994). Strategy as moral philosophy. *Strategic Management Journal, 15,* 191-213.

Slocum, J., & Hellriegel, D. (1983, July/August). A look at how managers' minds work. *Business Horizons,* pp. 58-68.

Sonnenfeld, J. (1988). *The hero's farewell: What happens when CEOs retire.* New York: Oxford University Press.

Sridharan, U. V. (1996). CEO influence and executive compensation. *Financial Review, 31,* 51-66.

Steindl-Rast, D. (1990). The shadow in Christianity. In C. Zweig & J. Abrams (Eds.), *Meeting the shadow* (pp. 131-133). New York: Tarcher/Putnam.

Stiles, J. (1994). Strategic alliances: Making them work. *Long Range Planning, 27*(4), 133-137.

Stewart, T. (1996). Why value statements don't work. *Fortune, 133*(11), 77-78.

Stuart, A. (1994). The vision thing. *CIO, 7*(20), 28-30.

Survey finds that employees view lack of trust as a problem in their organizations. (1995). *Quality Progress, 28*(10), 21-22.

Swindoll, C. (1993). *The quest for character.* New York: Zondervan.

Taggart, W., & Robey, D. (1981). Minds and managers: On the dual nature of human information processing and management. *Academy of Management Review, 6,* 187-195.

Terkel, S. (1974). *Working.* New York: Pantheon Books.

Tevlin, S. (1996, January/February). CEO incentive contracts, monitoring costs, and corporate performance. *New England Economic Review,* pp. 39-50.

Thompson, J. (1967). *Organizations in action.* New York: McGraw-Hill.

Torbert, W. (1996, August). *Who is in charge? The executive's spiritual journey.* Personal presentation at the National Academy of Management Meetings, Cincinnati, OH.

Townsend, B. (1996). Room at the top for women. *American Demographics, 18*(7), 28-37.

Truskie, S. (1990). *The president/CEO study: Leadership behaviors, skills, and attributes of executives who lead corporate 1000 companies.* Pittsburgh, PA: Management Science and Development.

Tuzzolino, F., & Armandi, B. (1981). A need-hierarchy framework for assessing corporate social responsibility. *Academy of Management Review, 6*(1), 21-28.

Vaill, P. (1991). *Managing as a performing art: New ideas for a world of chaotic change.* San Francisco: Jossey-Bass.

Vaill, P. (1996a). *Learning as a way of being.* San Francisco: Jossey-Bass.

Vaill, P. (1996b, August). *Who is in charge? The executive's spiritual journey.* Personal presentation at the National Academy of Management Meetings, Cincinnati, OH.

Van Buren, H. (1996, March). *Community, relationality, and the love of neighbor.* Presentation at the International Association for Business & Society, Santa Fe, NM.

Walck, C. (1992). Psychological type and management research: A review. *Journal of Psychological Type, 24,* 13-23.

Weber, M. (1920). *The Protestant ethic and the spirit of capitalism.* New York: Charles Scribner.

Weisbord, M., & Janoff, S. (1995). *Future search.* San Francisco: Berrett-Koehler.

Westley, F., & Mintzberg, H. (1989). Visionary leadership and strategic management. *Strategic Management Journal, 10* (special issue), 17-32.

Wheatley, M. (1994). *Leadership and the new science.* San Francisco: Berrett-Koehler.

Whitney, J. (1993). *The trust factor: Liberating profits and restoring corporate vitality.* New York: McGraw-Hill.

Whyte, D. (1994). *The heart aroused: Poetry and the preservation of soul in corporate America.* New York: Currency Doubleday.

Wilbur, K. (1990). Taking responsibility for your shadow. In C. Zweig & J. Abrams (Eds.), *Meeting the shadow* (pp. 273-277). New York: Tarcher/Putnam.

Wilson, I. (1992). Realizing the power of strategic vision. *Long Range Planning, 25*(5), 18-28.

Wuthnow, R. (1988). *The restructuring of American religion.* Princeton, NJ: Princeton University Press.

Yankelovich, D. (1981). *New rules: Searching for self-fulfillment in a world turned upside down.* New York: Random House.

Yearbook of American & Canadian Churches. (1997). New York: National Council of Churches.

Zaleznick, A. (1997). Real work. *Harvard Business Review, 75*(6), 53-63.

Zweig, C., & Abrams, J. (Eds.). (1990). *Meeting the shadow.* New York: Tarcher/Putnam.

Zweig, C., & Wolf, S. (1997). *Romancing the shadow: Illuminating the dark side of the soul.* New York: Ballantine.

Index

About the Author

William Q. Judge received his doctorate degree from the University of North Carolina at Chapel Hill in 1989. As Associate Professor of Management at the University of Tennessee, Knoxville, he teaches courses on strategic leadership for undergraduates, M.B.A. students, doctoral candidates, and executives. He has received several teaching awards and distinctions, including the Allan H. Keally Teaching Award. His research interests focus on value-laden aspects of the strategic management process; he has published articles in such journals as *Academy of Management Journal, Strategic Management Journal, Journal of Management, Journal of Management Studies, California Management Review,* and *Business and Society.* He currently serves on the editorial board of *Academy of Management Executive* and *Corporate Governance.*

In addition to his scholarly work, Judge has served on the board of directors of St. Mary's Health System since 1991. St. Mary's, a private, nonprofit, multihospital system in East Tennessee, is part of Catholic Healthcare Partners, Inc.—the sixth-largest health care delivery system in the United States. Prior to entering academe, he worked with strategic leaders at Armstrong World Industries, a *Fortune* 500 company. Also, he is a consultant on various strategic leadership issues for several corporate clients.

He lives in Knoxville with his wife, Sharon, and two children, Colin and Anastasia. He loves bicycling on the back roads of East Tennessee, sailing on any water that has a breeze, and playing with his children. His personal motto is *Aun Aprendo,* which translates to "I am still learning."